Wiggly Giggly Bible Learning Centers

FOR PRESCHOOLERS

Group
Loveland, Colorado

Wiggly, Giggly Bible Learning Centers for Preschoolers

Copyright © 2000 Group Publishing, Inc.

All rights reserved. No part of this book may be reproduced in any manner whatsoever without prior written permission from the publisher, except where noted in the text and in the case of brief quotations embodied in critical articles and reviews. For information write Permissions, Group Publishing, Inc., Dept. PD, P.O. Box 481, Loveland, CO 80539.

Visit our Web site: www.grouppublishing.com

Credits

Contributing Authors: Jacqui Baker, Sarah Macy Bohrer, Laurie Castañeda, Abby Flesch Connors, Diane Cory, Julie Lavendar, and Barbie Murphy

Editor: Lori Niles

Creative Development Editor: Linda A. Anderson

Chief Creative Officer: Joani Schultz

Copy Editor: Pam Klein

Cover Art Director: Jeff A. Storm

Cover Designer: Lisa Chandler

Cover Illustrator: Michael Morris

Art Director: Jean Bruns

Designers: Kari K. Monson and Jean Bruns

Computer Graphic Artist: Fred Schuth

Illustrator: Michael Morris

Production Manager: Peggy Naylor

Unless otherwise noted, Scripture taken from the HOLY BIBLE, NEW INTERNATIONAL VERSION®. Copyright © 1973, 1978, 1984 by International Bible Society. Used by permission of Zondervan Publishing House. All rights reserved.

Library of Congress Cataloging-in-Publication Data

Wiggly, giggly Bible learning centers for preschoolers.
   p. cm.
 ISBN 0-7644-2157-3 (alk. paper)
   1. Bible--Biography--Study and teaching (Preschool) 2. Christian education of preschool children. I. Group Publishing.
BS571.W549 2000
268'.432--dc21   99-087573

10 9 8 7 6 5 4 3 2 1   09 08 07 06 05 04 03 02 01 00

Printed in the United States of America.

Contents

Introduction 5

Noah 10
Genesis 6:1–9:17

Sarah 14
Genesis 18:1-15; 21:1-21

Rebekah 18
Genesis 24

Jacob 23
Genesis 25; 27–28; 32–33

Joseph 26
Genesis 37; 42–45

Miriam 30
Exodus 2:1-10

Moses 34
Exodus 3–14; 19–20

Joshua 38
Numbers 13:1–14:9

Rahab 42
Joshua 2

Deborah 47
Judges 4–5

Gideon 52
Judges 6–7

Samson 55
Judges 13–16

Ruth 59
Ruth 1–4

Hannah 63
1 Samuel 1:1–2:21

Samuel 67
1 Samuel 3

David 70
1 Samuel 17

Abigail 74
1 Samuel 25

Nathan 78
2 Samuel 7; 12

Solomon 82
1 Kings 3; 2 Chronicles 1–4; 9

Queen of Sheba 85
1 Kings 10:1-10, 13; 2 Chronicles 9:1-9, 12

Elijah 88
1 Kings 18

Naaman's Servant Girl 92
2 Kings 5:1-13

Esther 97
Esther 2–8

Daniel 100
Daniel 1; 3–6

Jonah 104
Jonah 1–4

Introduction

Welcome to the world of Old Testament Bible heroes—heroes whose stories will capture the attention and imagination of your wiggliest and giggliest preschoolers. *Wiggly, Giggly Bible Learning Centers for Preschoolers* will bring the Old Testament heroes to life as children interact with the stories through four fresh and creative centers for each character.

Wiggly, Giggly Bible Stories From the Old Testament begins your preschoolers' adventure with stories and activities to teach about twenty-five characters of epic proportions. This book of learning centers, a companion volume to *Wiggly, Giggly Bible Stories From the Old Testament*, can expand and extend those stories or augment stories from another source. Each group of centers is perfect for following up the lessons with extended opportunities for play and learning. You'll enhance your children's church, midweek program, vacation Bible school, or after-school program with these easy-to-use ideas to help your preschoolers fully experience and apply the principles taught in the stories.

At the beginning of each learning center, you will find a "To Do and To Notice" section that contains a simple explanation of the activity and explorative questions. Consider writing these explanations and questions on paper and posting them at the centers to assist the helpers as they move from center to center, encouraging children in their independent explorations.

A Look at the Learning Center Model

Here are some helpful pointers that will guide you to an exciting and successful experience using learning centers in your Christian education setting.

What exactly are learning centers?

Quite simply, learning centers are extended opportunities for children to explore the concepts you want them to learn through independent or small-group interaction. In a learning center approach, children...

- develop problem-solving skills,
- make decisions and choices about their own learning,

- experience cooperative learning with their peers,
- follow simple directions with little teacher assistance,
- learn through a hands-on, multi-sensory approach,
- stretch their imaginations to relate Bible stories to their experiences, and
- apply what they're learning from Bible stories to their lives.

Why should we use learning centers?

Have you ever had someone look in on your preschool classroom and ask, "Do they just play all the time? When are they going to learn something?"

Young children learn through play. Play allows children to explore the world around them and reveals children's interests as they are exposed to a variety of materials, selecting what they want to do. Play helps children develop emotionally, intellectually, physically, socially, and spiritually.

God made preschool children to learn best through hands-on, interactive experiences rather than through long times of listening to someone talk. Kids like to be given choices within an organized classroom. Learning centers can provide children with a variety of ways to explore a topic using all five senses and their burgeoning cooperative social skills. Learning centers match your children's need for play with your call to teach.

Who benefits from learning centers?

The children benefit because they have the opportunity to learn within the context of play…at their own pace…in small groups…with a hands-on approach.

You, the teacher, benefit because no matter how many children attend your class, you can create smaller, more manageable groups by providing learning centers. Divide + conquer = greater potential for learning.

Young children need to know that they are important and special individuals. Often we herd young children like sheep in a large flock. Some get lost in the shuffle. By creating smaller groups, we have the opportunity to focus on specific children. Learning centers allow children to interact and learn from their peers, while adults who participate with children in their play experiences gently help children stay focused.

How can learning centers be set up?

Almost any area can be set up for learning centers. The ideal area is spacious enough to allow all four centers to be set up. Some of the centers need more space than others. If all the centers are in one large room, low shelves or stacking bins make excellent dividers between centers. They can also be used to store the supplies needed in the center. Use cardboard screens made from refrigerator or dryer boxes, or mark off center areas with masking tape on the floor. You can also define a center using area rugs or neatly arranged tables.

Student Ratios

Each center should accommodate four to six preschoolers at a time. A center doesn't have to be full, but it should not be overcrowded. The four centers in each chapter will accommodate up to twenty-four children. If you have more children, set up identical centers, or add some centers that can be used from week to week, such as a cutting center, a stamping center, or a doll-play center. If you have too many centers, children may become worried about how to get to them all in the allotted time. If you have too few centers, the centers may get overcrowded.

Schedule

You may want to use the centers in conjunction with a circle time in which the whole group meets together for a Bible story summary and an introduction to the centers. The use of the circle along with the learning centers may take an entire class session, or it may be used for only a portion of the class time.

During the circle time, you may explain how each center ties in to the topic you're studying. Allow the children to select a center and to decide independently how long they will stay there, or assign children to small groups. These groups can then be assigned to specific centers where they remain until a signal is given for the groups to rotate to the next center. You'll need to establish signals for cleanup time and travel time.

If you have an hour with the children, you can offer centers in three twenty-minute blocks, four fifteen-minute blocks, or six ten-minute blocks. Try to allow time for children to visit at least half of the centers you have set up.

Some teachers use a different color to mark each center. The children are each given a ticket or nametag with the colors listed in a particular order, and the children go to the centers as indicated by the order of the colors.

Servants

It's helpful to have other adults serving as guides at each learning center. These guides should be encouraged to play along with the children and not to view themselves as traditional teachers. Remember—in centers the children have tasks, but much of the learning occurs by deciding how to complete the tasks and by what happens in the process. Whether adult guides stay in one center or move through several, the questions in the "To Do and To Notice" sections can help direct the children's activity into meaningful Bible-centered experiences. The goal is for the children to discover and learn as much as they can on their own. The guides are to assist when needed, not to lead or control the play.

Structure

Before center time, be sure to have the necessary materials ready at each center. The "What" and "Where" sections of each center give specific directions for setting up the materials in a way that allows children to get busy as soon as they arrive at the center. You will also need to determine the appropriate cleanup supplies for your situation and have them ready so that you can build responsibility by encouraging children to clean up at the end of their center time.

What kinds of learning centers can be offered?

As you plan learning centers, keep in mind that they are not just time fillers. The learning centers in this book are designed to tie in with the themes of the Bible stories, to reinforce the objectives of the lessons, and to allow children to practice developmentally appropriate skills.

Following is a list of some of the centers that can be offered.

- The **Blocks and Construction Center** allows children the opportunity to develop coordination as well as to express imagination in their play. Eye-hand coordination and spatial relationships are important to a child's overall development. Children often work together on block projects, so their social and cooperative skills are enhanced as well.
- The **Dramatic and Imaginative Play Center** helps children try on roles of people they hear about in stories. Children learn to express their imagination and socialize with their peers.
- The **Home and Life Skills Center** allows children to practice real-life applications of Bible themes and stories. Children connect Bible events to developmental skills such as dressing, cooking, or baby care.
- The **Small Motor Skills Center** gives children the opportunity to develop the muscles in their hands and fingers and to improve their eye-hand coordination. The children will use modeling dough, puzzles, beads, small blocks, and simple games at this center.
- The **Readiness Center** has activities that will connect to later academic skills, such as writing, counting, and classifying. At this center, children can also enhance their tactile discrimination as they learn to distinguish the difference between hard and soft, dull and sharp, or hot and cold.
- The **Prayer and Worship Center** provides an area for children to be quiet and to process what they're learning from the Bible and how their relationship with God is growing. Set out children's picture Bibles for kids to examine and enjoy. If a center leader is available, children can be guided to share what they're learning and to share prayer concerns they may have. This center can be enhanced with large pillows, beanbag chairs, or stuffed chairs to make a comfortable and cozy corner in your classroom.
- The **Arts and Crafts Center** allows children to express themselves creatively. Opportunities to improve tactile discrimination, visual memory, and small muscle control are also offered at this center. Ideally, children are encouraged to enjoy the process without the requirement of producing a perfect, finished product. Give children opportunities to express their creativity with a variety of art materials. Use small containers to store art supplies so they are readily available.
- The **Wet and Dry Center** provides children opportunities to experiment with pouring, measuring, mixing, and stirring. Children practice eye-hand coordination and spatial awareness. You can partially fill shallow containers such as cake pans or dishpans with wet or dry elements such as water, bubbles, rice, cornmeal, sand, and beans. Set out cups, measuring spoons, and funnels for children to use to scoop and pour. Be sure to have a broom and dustpan available for dry cleanup and a mop or heavy towel available for wet cleanup.
- The **Games Center** allows children to engage in activities that foster body awareness, coordination, and muscle strength. Games help children burn off energy and develop

social interaction skills. This center should be in a large area of the classroom and will probably be one of the noisiest centers. Often this center requires the most adult supervision.

• The **Listening and Music Center** gives children the opportunity to listen and respond. Provide a tape player or CD player, music, and musical instruments, and watch more independent fun begin. A great addition to this center is a listening post where headphones can be plugged in so that several children may hear the recordings without disturbing children in the surrounding centers.

• The **Science and Nature Center** gives children the opportunity to use their senses to explore the exciting world God has made. In this center, children might touch or sort nature items, get involved in an experiment, or predict outcomes.

• The **Cooking Center** allows children to follow a recipe and prepare a snack. This center helps children learn to follow directions, measure and pour, and explore their environment using their senses.

• The **Storytelling Center** gives children the opportunity to don costumes and put on dramas or use puppets to re-enact Bible stories. Preschool children love to express their imagination through make-believe and by pretending to put themselves into stories they have heard. In this center, children may use old clothing for costumes, make puppets from socks, and construct a puppet stage from a large cardboard box.

When can I get started?

Go for it now! Keep learning centers set up all the time in your classroom. The centers in this book are all simple enough to set up tomorrow. You'll get your wiggly, giggly preschoolers connected to the greatest stories of all time and the great God who works through the ages. And the next time someone asks you if the children are learning anything in your classroom, invite them to join you and the children for a Wiggly, Giggly Bible Learning Center approach to exploring and applying God's Word.

May God bless you as you use these centers to meet your preschool children where they are in their development and to help them grow socially, emotionally, mentally, physically, and spiritually alongside these Bible heroes.

Barbie Murphy

Barbie Murphy has been a director and teacher at Loveland Preschool in Loveland, Colorado, for sixteen years. She has contributed to more than ten Christian education resource books for preschoolers and is a former editor of Group's Hands-On Bible Curriculum™.

Noah Obeys God
Genesis 6:1–9:17

The story of Noah will help preschoolers learn about one man who became a hero because of his obedience to God. Noah's belief and trust in God sustained him as he prepared for impending disaster.

After the story, these centers will help children explore details of Noah's life and the character he displayed while acting in obedience to God.

Edible Ark
Cooking

To Do and To Notice—*Build an ark from cookies to learn about Noah's patience.*

As the children work, you can ask them these questions:
- **Why do you think God asked Noah to build such a big ark?**
- **How do you think Noah felt about living in a boat with so many different kinds of animals?**
- **What sorts of fun things would you do if you lived on a boat?**

What? You'll need approximately three butter cookies and a plastic knife for each child. (You may purchase cookies or make cookies from the recipe on page 108.) You'll also need a shallow box, frosting, and animal crackers.

Where? Set up a table covered with a plastic tablecloth in an area where the children can move around the table freely. Set the box in the center of the table. Place three cookies and a knife at each workspace, and put the frosting and animal crackers where children can easily reach them.

How? As you introduce the center, remind children that Noah built an ark large enough for all the animals. He had to wait a long time before it was time to use the ark. Tell the children that they are going to work together to create an "ark," but they'll have to wait awhile before they can eat the animal crackers it will hold.

Make sure children wash their hands before going to this center. Show them how to spread frosting on the back of the butter cookies and how to stick the cookies to the outside of the box. After they have stuck their cookies to the ark, they can sort through the animal crackers to find pairs and put them inside the ark. When all the animal crackers are in the ark, each child may choose three pairs to eat. Remove all the remaining animal crackers from the box so that the next group may sort them.

Two by Two

Games

To Do and To Notice—*Play a pair-matching game to remind kids that Noah had to find two of each kind of animal.*

As the children work, you can ask them these questions:
- **How hard is it to find two cards that match?**
- **Which animals do you think were the easiest to get into the ark? the hardest?**
- **Which animals do you think were Noah's favorites? Which are your favorite animals?**

What? You'll need to cut two 2x2-inch squares from each of eight different colors of construction paper. Glue each square on one-half of an index card.

Where? Choose an area of the room where there is enough floor space for four to six children to sit in a circle. Mix up the cards and place them on the floor, face down, in four rows of four.

How? Have the children sit in a circle around the rows of cards. Begin with the child wearing the most red. Let that child select any two cards to turn face up. If he or she selects two cards that don't match, the cards are placed face down and the child to the left gets a turn. If the cards match, the child keeps the cards and tries to name an animal that is the same color as the matching cards. Continue playing until all the cards are matched. Then the children can lay them face down for the next group of kids.

Around the Corner

Set out books with color photos or color drawings of animals so that children can look at the colors of different animals.

Floating Boats

Wet and Dry

To Do and To Notice—*Float toy boats to learn about different weather forces that may have affected Noah and the ark.*

As the children work, you can ask them these questions:
- **What kind of weather is most difficult for a boat?**
- **How do you think Noah felt about God being in charge of his boat?**

What? You'll need a small, inflatable pool (allowing four to six children to work together) or a large pan filled with water (allowing children to take turns at the water), a plastic tablecloth, and several foam cups with the tops cut off or plastic boats. You'll also need a straw for each child.

Where? Spread a plastic tablecloth on the floor away from any electrical outlets. Place the pool or pan in the center of the plastic tablecloth for easy cleanup.

How? As you introduce the center, talk about different kinds of weather Noah might have experienced during his time on the ark. Give each child a toy boat. Let the children put their boats in the water. Encourage them to explore forces that will move the boats, by blowing air at them, using a straw to blow bubbles in the water, pushing the boats with the straws, making whirlpools, and using other creative methods. Encourage children to use weather terms such as calm, stormy, or windy to describe the conditions around their boats.

Rainbows of Promise
Science and Nature

To Do and To Notice—*Create rainbows on transparencies and see how the rainbows change when projected onto the wall.*

As the children work, you can ask them these questions:
- **What is your favorite color of the rainbow?**
- **How do you think Noah felt when he saw the very first rainbow?**
- **What is special about a promise?**

What? For each child, you'll need half of a transparency sheet and a copy of the rainbow on page 13. You'll also need tape, nontoxic erasable markers in all colors of the rainbow, an overhead projector, and a blank wall space or a sheet of white poster board mounted on a wall.

Where? Set up an overhead projector where it can be easily moved to change the appearance of the projected images. Set a table and four to six chairs nearby. Place a copy of the rainbow handout at each workspace, and tape the transparency over the top to hold the image steady.

How? As you introduce the center, remind the children that God sent a rainbow as a promise to Noah that he would never flood the whole earth again. Have the children use the photocopies of the rainbow as guides to create their own rainbows on transparencies with the markers. As children finish their rainbows, they may place them on the overhead projector and turn on the projector light to discover what happens to the images. Children can work together to explore overlapping images and different placements. Guide children to discover how to make the rainbows bigger, smaller, brighter, and darker.

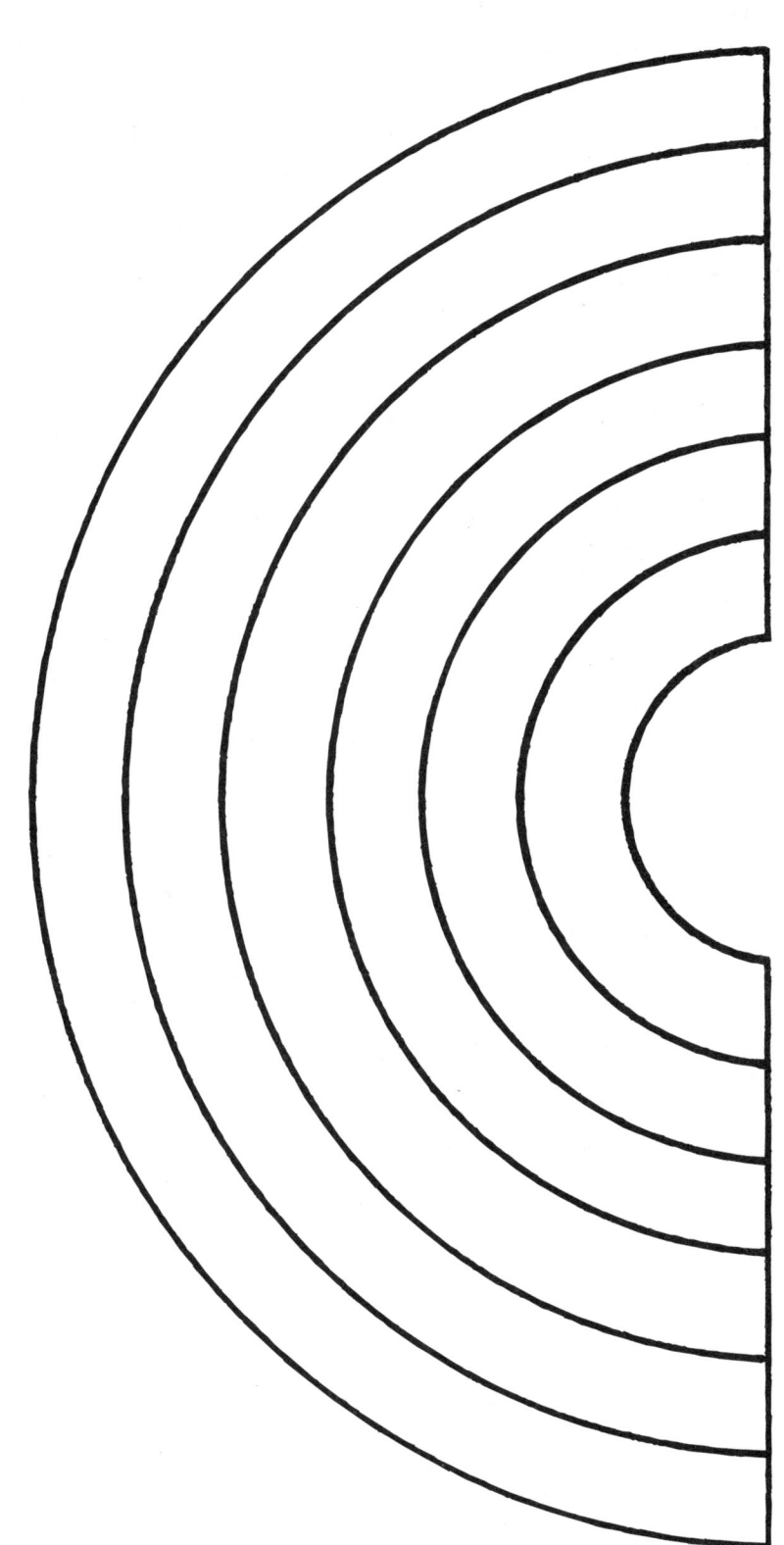

Sarah
Genesis 18:1-15; 21:1-21

A ninety-year-old woman having a baby? The thought is laughable! But Sarah was soon to discover that nothing is too hard for God. Although Sarah doubted God's promise of a son, her story offers us a clear example of God's promises coming true. In the face of what seemed impossible, God used Sarah to fulfill a powerful covenant.

After telling the story, use these centers to help preschoolers delight in the surprises of God and learn that nothing is too hard for him.

A Big Surprise
Listening and Music

To Do and To Notice—*Experience feelings of surprise like those Sarah felt when she heard that she would have a baby.*

Ask these questions after the children have listened to the tape:
- **How did it feel to hear the big noises? Was it scary? funny? Did the noises make you jump?**
- **Which was the strangest noise on the tape? Why?**
- **How do you think Sarah felt when she heard that she was going to have a baby? Do you think it was a big surprise?**
- **What's the most surprising news you've ever gotten?**

What? You'll need a tape recorder and a "surprise tape" for this activity. Begin by recording twenty seconds of silence, then loudly clang two pot lids together. After twelve more seconds of silence, blow a whistle. Alternate twelve-second periods of silence with the following noises: ice cubes dropping into a plastic dish, a wooden spoon banging on a table, slightly cupped hands clapping, and a dog barking (or an imitation of a dog barking). You may also wish to try using a hair dryer, ringing a bell, slamming a door, or shaking a sheet of aluminum foil. Have fun making this tape!

Where? Children will need a space where they can sit in a circle on the floor away from the other centers to prevent other children from hearing the tape.

How? Show the children how to operate the cassette recorder. Then allow the children to listen to the tape and experience the loud surprises. If you have time, play the tape a second time and ask the children if they can identify the sounds.

Sarah's Laughter
Sensory Exploration

To Do and To Notice—*Explore different forms and expressions of laughter.*

As the children work, you can ask them these questions:
- **Sarah laughed when she heard that she would have a baby. How do you think her laughter sounded?**
- **Is a quiet laugh hard to hear? Do you think a laugh could be too quiet for God to hear?**
- **When you laugh, what parts of your body move? Is it just your mouth? Do you feel your shoulders move? your belly?**
- **What is your favorite type of laugh?**

What? You'll need a "laughter sign" for this activity. On a piece of poster board, display a picture of a person laughing, either drawn or clipped from a magazine.

Where? Designate a comfortable, roomy space for children to sit on the floor.

How? Remind the children that when God promised Sarah she'd have a baby, Sarah laughed. She laughed so much that she and Abraham even named the baby Isaac, which means "laughter." Hand the laughter sign to one of the children. Explain to the kids that whoever is holding the sign may laugh in whatever way he or she wishes. It might be a soft laugh, a loud laugh, or something else. After each laugh, the other children can try to imitate the sound. Pass the sign to another child who can then laugh in a different way. Encourage kids to experiment with different kinds of laughter. Have them try loud laughs, quiet laughs, high and low laughs, slow and quick laughs, silly laughs, and whatever else they can think of!

Abraham and Sarah's Celebration Tent
Arts and Crafts

To Do and To Notice—*Decorate a paper tent like the one Abraham and Sarah shared.*

As the children work, you can ask them these questions:
- **Why didn't Sarah believe that she would have a baby?**
- **How do you think Sarah felt when her son was born?**
- **Tell about a time you waited a long time for something you wanted. What happened when you got it?**

What? You'll need newspaper, 6x8-inch pieces of brown paper grocery sacks, crayons, markers, glue or paste, and confetti or sequins.

Where? Set up a table with four to six chairs around it. Cover the workspace with newspaper. Put a piece of brown paper at each workspace. Place the rest of the supplies on the table where they are accessible to all the children.

How? Show the children how to fold their pieces of paper in half widthwise to make tents that can stand up. Remind the children that Abraham and Sarah celebrated when their son was born. They may have even decorated their tent. Have the children decorate their tents for a celebration, using the crayons, markers, confetti, and sequins. Encourage them to be creative and use lots of different colors and materials.

You may wish to copy the following rhyme for the children to take home to review with their parents:

Sarah laughed in her tent one morn, but one year later her baby was born!

Find the Angels
Arts and Crafts

To Do and To Notice—*Paint a picture to discover that angels can look like ordinary people.*

As the children work, you can ask them these questions:
- **Why do you think God sent these special angels to Abraham and Sarah?**
- **Why do you think they didn't tell Abraham and Sarah that they were really angels from God?**
- **If angels came to your house for lunch, what would you serve them?**

Around the Corner

Allow the children to experiment by using a white crayon to draw or write whatever they wish on another piece of paper, and then have children paint over their drawings. This activity could also be done with a partner, with one child using a crayon to create a secret picture for another child to discover by painting over it.

What? You'll need photocopies of the "Hidden Angels" handout on page 17, a white crayon, blue watercolor paint, paintbrushes, water, and newspaper or a plastic tablecloth.

Where? Set up a table with four to six chairs around it, and cover it with newspaper or with a plastic tablecloth. Before class use the white crayon to draw a halo over the head of one of the four people pictured on each of the photocopies. Place one of these prepared photocopies and a paintbrush at each workspace. Place the rest of the supplies so that all the children can reach them.

How? Remind the children that the angels who visited Abraham and Sarah looked just like everyone else they knew. Have the children look at the pictures on the photocopies and guess which one is an angel. Then have them paint watercolors over all the characters, being careful to cover the whole paper with paint. The white crayon will resist the watercolors, allowing children to identify the angels on their papers.

Hidden Angels

Rebekah, the Willing Servant
Genesis 24

Rebekah was the daughter of Abraham's nephew. Abraham sent his servant back to Abraham's hometown to find a wife among his relatives for his son Isaac. Through God's guidance, the servant was drawn to Rebekah's willingness to care for him and his animals. He found out that she was one of Abraham's relatives and went to meet her parents. Rebekah's willingness to go with the servant overcame her parents' reluctance to send her so far away, and her parents allowed her to marry Isaac.

After children hear the story, these centers will help them discover and understand the importance of serving others willingly and cheerfully, as Rebekah did when she served Abraham's servant and his camels.

Camel Puppets
Storytelling

To Do and To Notice—*Create camel puppets and experience the story of Rebekah from a camel's point of view.*

As the children work, you can ask them these questions:
- **What do you think the camels who traveled to meet Rebekah went through to get there?**
- **How do you think the camels felt after Rebekah gave them water?**
- **How do you think the camels would describe Rebekah? What kind of person was she?**
- **Have you ever seen a real camel?**

What? You'll need brown paper lunch bags, photocopies of the camel features on page 19, scissors, crayons or markers, and glue.

Where? Set up a table with four to six chairs around it. Place a lunch bag and a photocopy of the camel features at each workspace. Place the rest of the supplies where they are accessible to each child.

How? Have children color the camel features and cut them out. Younger children may need help cutting. Then kids can glue the camel faces onto the paper bags to create camel puppets. Children can insert their hands and work the puppets to make them "talk."

Encourage the children to use the puppets to tell a partner about Rebekah and the camels. Let the children use their imagination to show what the camels did when they were hot and thirsty, when they were tired, when they were drinking, or when they were sleeping.

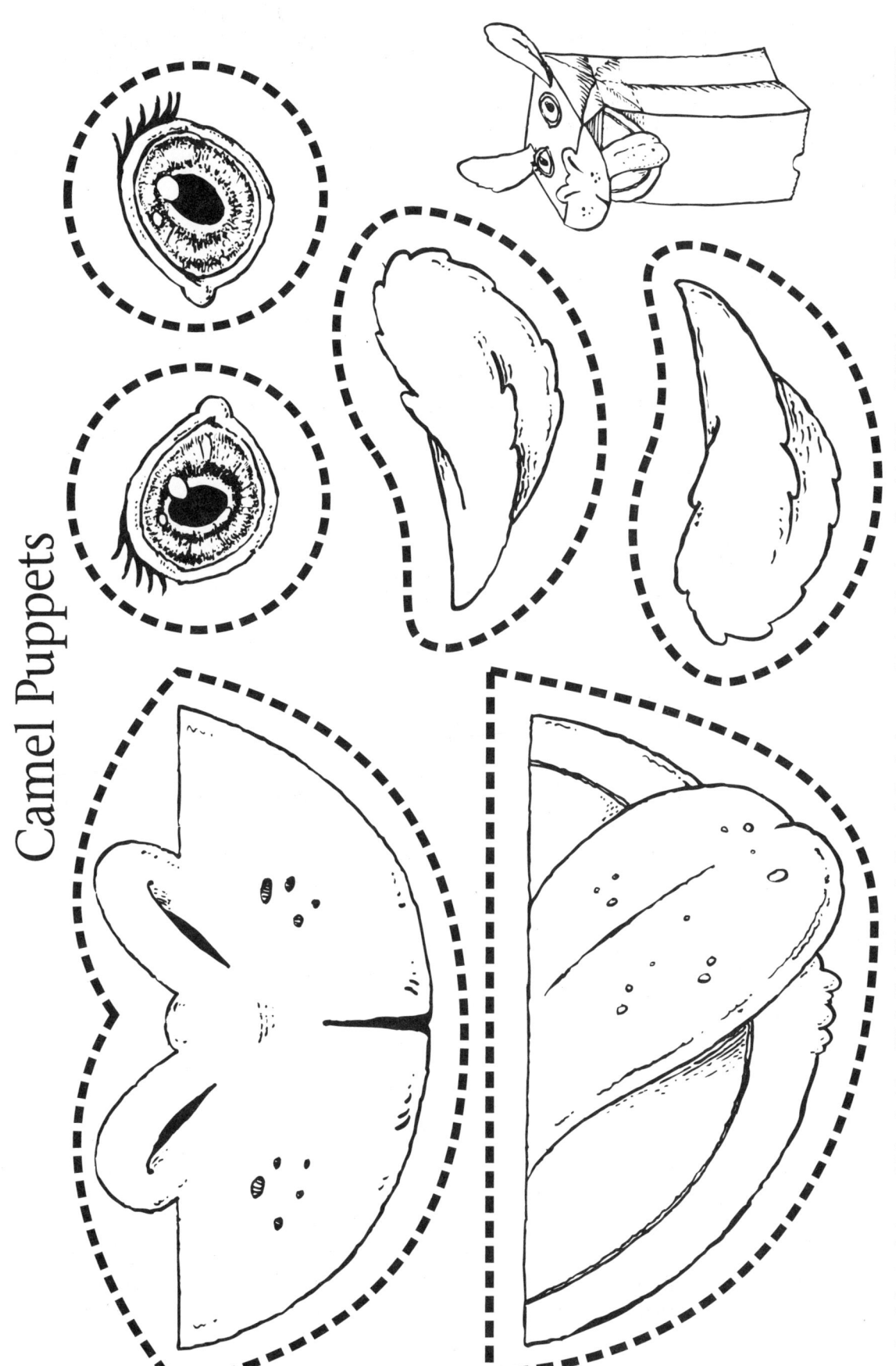

Rebekah's Smile
Cooking

> **To Do and To Notice**—*Make tasty snacks to remember Rebekah's friendly smile.*

As the children work, you can ask them these questions:
- **How do you feel when people smile as they help you?**
- **What if they're grumpy and frowning as they help you?**
- **Who would like to see your smile today? Tell us about him or her.**

What? You'll need paper towels, paper plates, plastic knives, pita bread halves, strawberry jam, and mini-marshmallows.

Where? Choose a table near a sink so children can wash their hands before and after working in the center. Put a paper plate, a plastic knife, and a pita half at each workspace. Put the other supplies on the table where all kids can reach them.

How? As you introduce the center, remind the children that Rebekah was kind and most likely smiled at Abraham's servant. Show the children how to spread strawberry jam on top of their pita halves and arrange some marshmallow "teeth" to make Rebekah's smile. Before eating their snacks, encourage the children to talk about kind acts that make them smile.

Gifts of Jewelry
Arts and Crafts

> **To Do and To Notice**—*Create jewelry from foil to remember the gifts Abraham's servant brought to Rebekah.*

As the children work, you can ask them these questions:
- **What are some special gifts you have received?**
- **How do you think Rebekah felt when she saw all the gifts the servant brought?**
- **How do you think Rebekah's family felt about her marrying someone who lived so far away?**

Around the Corner

For more fun, provide a mirror so the children can see themselves wearing their new jewelry. You may also wish to provide some brightly colored silk scarves to add to the effect.

What? You'll need pieces of aluminum foil and white glue.

Where? Put the foil in a place where children can sit comfortably on the floor.

How? As you introduce this center, explain that Abraham's servant brought a lot of jewelry and other fine gifts to give to Rebekah and her family. Show the children some of the ways to twist and shape different amounts of aluminum foil. Show kids how to make beads to string on foil ropes or decorative pieces to glue on folded foil strips. Have the children tell about different kinds of jewelry they have seen. Then allow the children to shape the foil into rings, necklaces, earrings, and other kinds of jewelry. Let kids dress each other in this beautiful jewelry.

Water for the Camels
Readiness

To Do and To Notice—*Color pictures of camels and "water" the camels.*

As the children work, you can ask them these questions:
- **It isn't taking very long for you to make this picture. How long do you think it took Rebekah to give water to ten camels?**
- **Have you ever done a job that took a long time? Tell about it.**
- **How can God help us to be cheerful helpers as Rebekah was?**

What? You'll need photocopies of the camel faces on page 22, crayons, a damp sponge, a paper plate, washable blue paint, and paper towels for kids to wipe their hands on.

Where? Set up a table and four to six chairs. Put a copy of the camel faces and some crayons at each workspace. Place the damp sponge on the paper plate, and pour some blue paint on the sponge to create a "stamp pad." Place this where all the children can reach it.

How? As you introduce the center, explain to the children that they are going to give ten camels some water, just as Rebekah did. First have the children color the camels. Then have each child dip each finger (one finger at a time) in the blue paint on the sponge and make a fingerprint on the paper under each camel face. Afterward, they can count their ten fingers and the ten fingerprints to make sure they have given each camel some water.

Water for the Camels

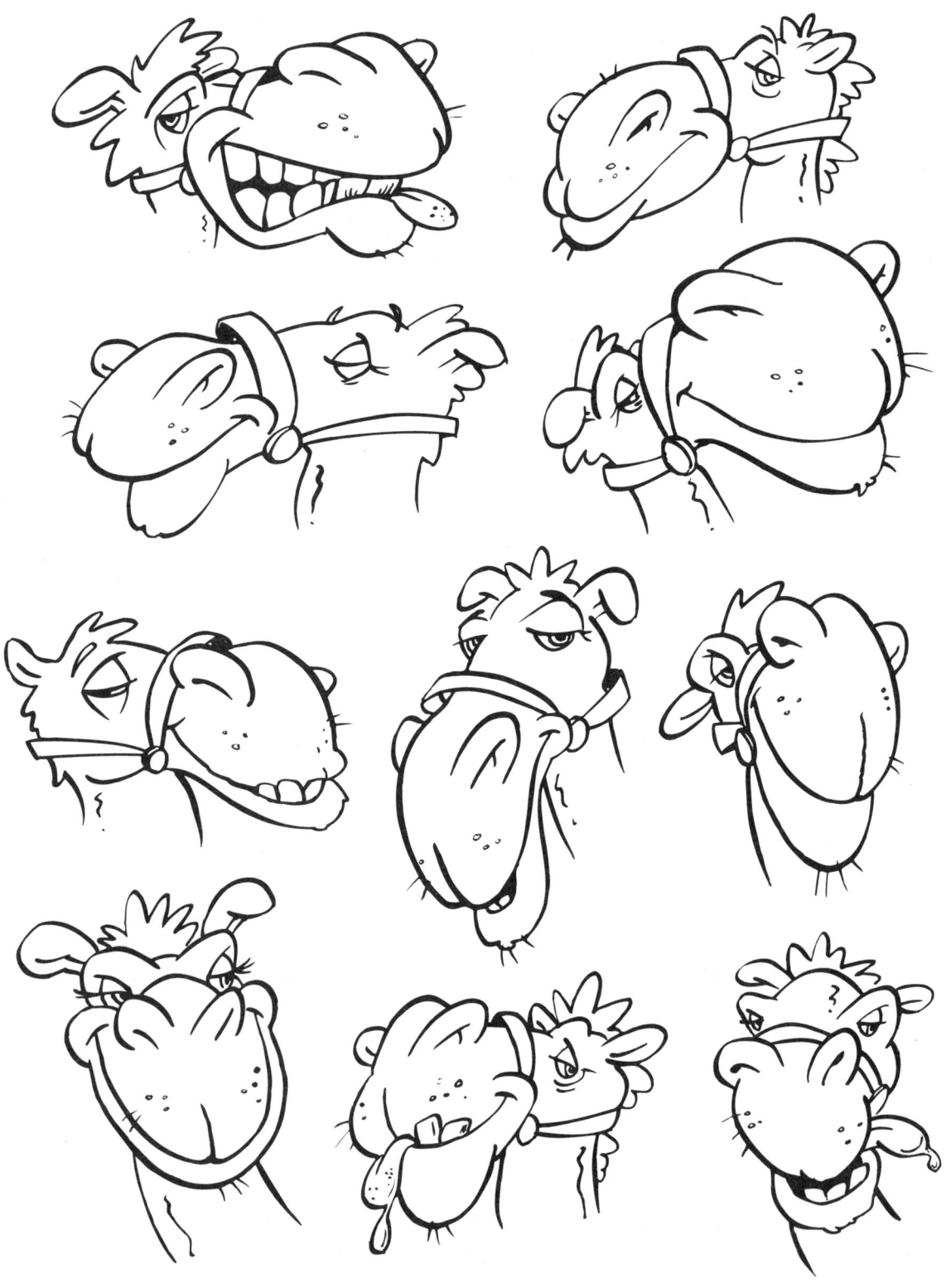

Permission to photocopy this handout from *Wiggly, Giggly Bible Learning Centers for Preschoolers* granted for local church use. Copyright © Group Publishing, Inc., P.O. Box 481, Loveland, CO 80539.

Jacob—Forgiven Father Israel

Genesis 25; 27–28; 32–33

Jacob, the deceiver, became forgiven Israel, the father of the Hebrew nation. Although he sinned against God and his own brother, Jacob received forgiveness when he sincerely expressed sorrow for his wrongdoing.

After telling the story, use these centers to help preschoolers understand repentance and forgiveness as they learn more about Jacob's life.

Don't Stay Mad
Home and Life Skills

To Do and To Notice—*Experience the uncomfortable feeling of maintaining an angry expression and the joy and relief of smiling.*

After this activity, you can ask the children these questions:
- **Why is it hard to keep an angry face?**
- **How did you feel when the game was over and you could smile again?**
- **How does it feel to be angry?**
- **How does it feel to forgive?**
- **How do you think Jacob and Esau felt after Esau forgave Jacob?**

What? You'll need a stand-up or full-length mirror, wipe-off markers, and paper towels.

Where? Place the mirror so children can comfortably look into it as they sit. Place four to six chairs around the mirror.

How? As you introduce the center, explain that Jacob and his brother Esau stayed angry for a long time because of problems they had with each other. Have the children look in the mirror and make faces they might make if they felt angry. Tell children to notice the position of their mouths and eyebrows. Let each child in the center choose a partner. Have one child in each pair hold an angry expression as long as he or she can while the partner draws around the image on the mirror with a wipe-off marker. After each child has had a turn maintaining an angry expression, have the partners sit in chairs facing each other. Tell them to see who can hold the expression longer without laughing. Allow the children to draw other expressions on the mirror, too.

Fair Pairs

Readiness

To Do and To Notice—*Match up similar objects as a reminder that, though Jacob and Esau were twins, they were very different from each other.*

After the activity, you can ask the children these questions:
- **How are the two parts of each of these pairs alike? How is each part different?**
- **How were Jacob and Esau alike? How were they different?**
- **Who in your family are you like? In what ways?**

What? You'll need pairs of similar but not identical items such as plastic fruit and real fruit, two unmatched socks, two mismatched shoes, two kinds of vegetables, two styles of earrings, two different mugs, two pieces of paper of different colors, a wooden spoon and a teaspoon, and a book and a magazine. You'll also need a laundry basket.

Where? Set the laundry basket filled with all the items on the floor in an area where children can move around freely.

How? As you introduce this center, remind the children that Jacob and his brother Esau were twins, but they were very different from each other. Help the children review some of the traits of both Jacob and Esau. You might want to have children do this activity in pairs. Encourage the children to explore the contents of the laundry basket and to work together to find pairs that are similar but not the same. The children may have some differences of opinion. Encourage them to explain to each other the reasons for their opinions. After they have grouped the items in pairs, they can extend their logical thinking by combining pairs that have similarities (such as pairing the mugs with the spoons because both are kept in the kitchen).

Jacob and Esau in the Desert

Dramatic and Imaginative Play

To Do and To Notice—*Use toy figures to act out the story of Jacob and Esau in the desert.*

After the children act out the story, you can ask them these questions:
- **Why do you think Esau forgave Jacob?**
- **Why did Jacob bring gifts to Esau?**
- **What kind of gifts do you like to receive?**

What? You'll need newspaper, a large roasting pan or another shallow container filled with a 1-inch layer of cornmeal, and assorted human and animal figures.

Where? Cover an area of the floor with newspaper, and place the roasting pan in the center of the newspaper. Make sure there is enough space for the children to move freely around the roasting pan. Set the human and animal figures nearby.

How? As you introduce the center, remind children of Jacob and Esau's meeting in the desert. Remind them that Jacob was forgiven by Esau. Explain to the children that they can act out the story of Jacob and Esau using the figures you've provided. Encourage the children to imagine the conversation between Jacob and Esau. Allow the children lots of freedom in how they play out the story.

Jacob's Animals
Cooking

To Do and To Notice—*Create an edible scene of animals walking through the desert to illustrate Jacob's gift to Esau.*

As the children work, you can ask them these questions:
- **What are your favorite animals?**
- **What kind of animal would you like to receive as a gift?**
- **How do you feel when someone forgives you?**

What? You'll need paper towels, graham crackers, plastic knives, plastic spoons, small resealable bags, vanilla frosting, and animal crackers.

Where? Set up four to six chairs around a table. Set a paper towel at each workspace. Place two graham crackers, a plastic knife, a plastic spoon, and a resealable bag on each paper towel. Place the frosting and the animal crackers where they are accessible to each child.

How? Explain to the children that they will be creating an edible desert scene. Remind them that Jacob and Esau met in the desert and that Jacob sent gifts ahead. Show the children how to use a plastic knife to spread frosting on a graham cracker. Show them how to put another graham cracker inside a plastic bag, seal the bag, and pound the cracker into crumbs to make "sand." Sprinkle the sand over the frosting on the other cracker. Then choose several animal crackers to stand in the frosting  as a reminder of the animals Jacob gave to Esau. When the snacks are made, the children may eat them. Yum! Leave your model at the center so that children can remember how to make the scene.

Joseph and His Brothers
Genesis 37; 42–45

The story of Joseph can encourage little ones to forgive one another and to trust God to turn bad into good. Although his brothers treated him poorly, Joseph forgave them and provided for them during a seven-year famine. In the end, Joseph acknowledged that God, more than the malicious acts of his brothers, sent him to Egypt.

After telling the story, use these centers to help your preschoolers understand more about Joseph and learn that they, too, can trust God to work in all situations.

A Beautiful Coat
Arts and Crafts

To Do and To Notice—*Create a coat from a paper bag to discover how special Joseph's coat was.*

As the children work, you can ask them these questions:
- **Why do you think Joseph's brothers were upset that they didn't have a coat like Joseph's?**
- **How do you think Joseph felt when his brothers took his coat away from him?**
- **When have you had a fight with your brothers or sisters? How did you work it out?**

What? For each child, you'll need a large paper bag cut into the shape of a coat (see the margin diagram) and a glue stick. Also set out small scraps of fabric, glitter glue, markers, ribbon, lace, sequins, and craft jewels.

Where? Set up a table and chairs to create four to six workspaces.

How? As you introduce this center, remind children of the special gift Joseph's father gave to him. Allow kids to decorate their paper-bag coats by coloring and gluing on the materials of their choice. Encourage kids to decorate both the front and back of their coats.

Hide-and-Seek Joseph
Games

To Do and To Notice—*Hide a doll as a reminder of how Joseph's brothers tried to hide him.*

As the children work, you can ask them these questions:
- **How did it feel to hide the doll?**
- **How did it feel to be the only one who didn't know where the doll was hidden?**
- **How do you think Reuben, Joseph's oldest brother, felt when he couldn't find Joseph?**

What? You'll need a small doll dressed in bright clothes.

Where? Choose an area of the room that has a lot of good places to hide a doll.

How? As you introduce the center, remind the children of how Joseph was lost to his brothers. Have one child close his or her eyes while the others at this center hide the doll. When kids have finished, encourage the waiting child to look for the doll. Let each child have a turn to be the seeker, as Reuben looked for Joseph in the story.

Moving to Egypt
Dramatic and Imaginative Play

To Do and To Notice—*Travel in boxes to imagine what it might have been like for Joseph's family to travel to Egypt in carts.*

As the children work, you can ask them these questions:
- **How did you feel being pushed around the room in a box?**
- **How do you think Joseph's family felt riding all the way to Egypt in carts?**
- **How do you think Joseph's dad felt knowing that he was going to see his son again?**

What? You'll need several boxes that are big enough for kids to sit in. You'll also need bathrobes and towels to create Bible costumes.

Where? Designate an open space in which the children can move freely.

How? Let children dress in the Bible costumes and let them pretend to be Joseph's family. Encourage them to talk about what they think will happen when they get to Egypt. Have children take turns slowly pushing and pulling each other in the box "carts," as oxen or donkeys might have pulled the cart. If there are extra clothes, the kids may want to pack them in the boxes, too.

Brotherly Gifts

Storytelling

> **To Do and To Notice**—*Use puppets to tell the story of Joseph giving gifts to his brothers.*

As the children work, you can ask them these questions:
- **Why do you think Joseph gave his brothers pretty, new clothes?**
- **How do you think Joseph's brothers felt when they were given new clothes?**
- **How do you feel when you are given something new?**

What? You'll need enough copies of the figures on page 29 for each child to create one puppet (cut apart each of the four pictures), crayons, scissors, glue, and one craft stick per person.

Where? Set a table on its side in a corner of the room to create a puppet stage. You'll also need to set up an art table nearby for four to six children to create puppets.

How? Let each child color a different figure. Show children how to glue each figure to a stick to create a puppet. When all the children have finished, have them move to the puppet stage and work together using the puppets to retell the story of how Joseph gave gifts to his brothers.

Brotherly Gifts

Big Sister Miriam
Exodus 2:1-10

Miriam was Moses' big sister. We find her for the first time in the Bible as she watched over her little brother and experienced God's care and mercy for Moses and for the family. She is known for her trust in God and the joyful praise she gave to God when he freed the Israelites from Egypt.

Miriam hid in the reeds and watched as her baby brother floated down the river. The whole incident must have been traumatic for her. Yet the experience must have strengthened her for what was to come. After telling the story, use these centers to help your preschoolers explore Miriam's story and learn more about the events that helped her to become the first female worship leader recorded in God's Word.

River Float
Dramatic and Imaginative Play

To Do and To Notice—*Pretend to be Miriam as she watched baby Moses float down the river.*

As the children work, you can ask them these questions:
- **Why do you think Miriam followed baby Moses' basket along the river as he floated along?**
- **How do you think Miriam felt as she watched her brother float away from her?**
- **Who else was watching Moses float down the river?**

What? You'll need a blue flat bedsheet, blocks to build the riverbank, a small doll, and a scarf. Use double-stick tape to attach a piece of wax paper to the outside surface of a breadbasket. Place one or two bricks inside the basket, and cover them with dry grass.

Where? You'll need a large, open area where the children can work. Keep all the supplies together at one end of the area, and let the children pick them up as they're ready to use them.

How? As you introduce the center, direct the children to make long lines of blocks several feet apart to form riverbanks. Then show children how to lay the sheet across the top. Have kids choose one child to be Miriam and to wear the scarf. The rest of the children will help move baby Moses down the river as Miriam follows along the bank. Explain that Miriam's job is to make sure the baby is safe. When everything is ready, have Miriam place baby Moses in the basket, and put the basket "in the water" (at one end of the sheet). The rest of the children will take their places on either side of the river and lift the sheet slightly to move the basket along. The wax paper and the weight of the bricks will help the basket glide along the river. If the basket tips over, have Miriam place the doll back inside the basket. Point out that, fortunately, the real baby Moses did not fall out into the river, but that Miriam was watching closely to make sure he was safe as he floated down the river. Let the children take turns being Miriam.

Tar Baskets

Arts and Crafts

To Do and To Notice—*Create baskets that resemble the basket Moses was placed in.*

As the children work, you can ask them these questions:
- **Who do you think might have helped Moses' mother make the tar basket for Moses?**
- **If you had been Miriam, how would you have felt about helping your mother with this job?**
- **Why do you think Miriam was willing to put her baby brother in the river?**

What? You'll need excelsior or Spanish moss from the floral department of a craft store (about one package for each group of four to six children), a berry basket for each child, white glue mixed with black tempera paint (three parts glue to one part tempera paint), three soft-margarine tub lids, cotton swabs, and a plastic tablecloth to cover the work area.

Where? Set up a table with four to six chairs around it, and cover the table with the plastic tablecloth. Put a margarine tub lid with about one tablespoon of the black glue between every two workspaces. Place the rest of the supplies where they are accessible to all the children. Display the model basket in the center.

How? Before class, make a model for this activity. Push Spanish moss into the holes inside of a basket. Paint some of the black glue on the outside of the basket, and let it dry thoroughly. As you introduce the center, tell the children they will be making baskets covered with a substance that looks a lot like the pitch Miriam's mother used to make the basket watertight for baby Moses. Make a separate basket as you show the children how to poke the excelsior or Spanish moss into the holes in the berry baskets. Show children how to carefully dip their cotton swabs into the black glue and dab it all over the outside of the basket. Encourage the children to pretend to be Miriam helping her mother make the basket for baby Moses.

Laundry-Basket Love
Home and Life Skills

To Do and To Notice—*Pretend to bathe baby Moses and prepare him for his floating trip in the basket.*

As the children work, you can ask them these questions:
- **How do you think Miriam and her mother felt as they got Moses ready before sending him down the river?**
- **What do you think Miriam was thinking about as she helped with the baby?**
- **Have you ever helped take care of a baby? What was it like?**

What? You'll need four to six baby dolls, a baby blanket for each doll, a small laundry basket, a plastic bathtub for infants, washcloths, and baby soap. Put a small amount of water in the plastic bathtub.

Where? If you have a housekeeping center, set the items there. If not, place a plastic tablecloth on the floor and set the supplies on it.

How? Let each child select a doll and pretend that he or she is Miriam, helping to give baby Moses a bath before his trip down the river. After the children have bathed their baby Moses dolls, let them wrap the dolls in blankets and put the dolls inside the laundry basket. Then the children may unwrap the dolls and repeat the process of pretending to wash baby Moses.

Grass in a Pan
Wet and Dry

To Do and To Notice—*Pretend to float baby Moses among the reeds to retell the story of how Miriam cared for him.*

As the children work, you can ask them these questions:
- **Do you have a brother or sister? What do you love about him or her?**
- **Why do you think the reeds were a good place for Miriam to hide?**
- **What would be fun about being in the reeds?**

What? You'll need a small, inflated swimming pool containing about two inches of water; green Easter grass or gift-bag filler; small plastic dishes or lids; a girl doll; 4x4-inch pieces of cotton cloth; and chenille wires.

Where? Choose a place in the room where the pool can be safely set up. Put water and the Easter grass in the pool. Put the rest of the supplies nearby.

How? Show the children how to make a baby Moses doll by rolling up a piece of cotton cloth and twisting a piece of chenille wire around it. Allow the children to float their babies in the different containers you've provided. Explain that the girl doll represents Miriam. Let children experiment with the doll to see if they can make it stand. As they play, encourage them to retell details of the story and to explain what finally happened.

Moses Leads God's People
Exodus 3–14; 19–20

Moses is one of the best examples in the Bible of obedience to God. Not only did Moses follow God's command to lead his people out of slavery, but he also set a wonderful example of faithfulness for all of us to follow.

After telling the story of Moses, use these centers to help your preschoolers learn how wonderful it is to know God, the mighty deliverer.

Rolling Back the Sea
Dramatic and Imaginative Play

To Do and To Notice—*Pretend to be Moses holding up his staff and watching God roll back the sea for the people of Israel to pass through.*

As the children work, you can ask them these questions:
- **What happens when people walk into water that is over their heads?**
- **How do you think God's people felt when God opened the sea for them?**
- **What does the story of the parting of the Red Sea tell us about God?**

What? You'll need belts and robes or towels to use as costumes, a tree branch to represent a staff, and two blue blankets or sheets.

Where? Choose and area of the room with enough floor space for children to spread out and move around freely. Place all the supplies in this area.

How? As you introduce this center, walk through the sequence one time with the children; then they will be ready to play on their own. Say: **The Bible tells us that when God rolled back the sea, he did it by stirring up a big wind. God can do anything!** Let the children spread out the blue blankets side by side to form a sea. Have the children select one child to be Moses, who will hold up the staff. As soon as the child holds up the staff, the rest of the children can work together to separate the blankets, forming a path between them, as they make the sounds of a howling wind. Then have all the children follow Moses across the "dry land." Have kids spread the blankets out again and choose new characters to play the game.

Around the Corner
Station an adult at the center to operate a fan so that the children can experience the mighty wind that rolled back the sea!

Hero Fingers
Storytelling

To Do and To Notice—*Use hand puppets to act out the story of Moses rolling back the sea.*

As the children work, you can ask them these questions:
- **What do you think might have happened if God had not rolled back the sea?**
- **What do you think you would have said if you had seen the parting of the Red Sea?**
- **Who would you have wanted to take with you if you had walked between the walls of water?**

What? You'll need a blanket, three pairs of blue mittens or socks, and three pairs of white or cream-colored mittens or socks with a face drawn on each.

Where? Set up a puppet stage by covering a table with a blanket. Allow plenty of space behind the table for the children to move around.

How? As you introduce the center, show the children how to put the blue socks or mittens on their hands. Choose a child to put a pair of white socks or mittens on his or her hands and stand in front of you. Explain that the white mittens are Miriam and Moses. Reach your arms around the child and put your hands (palms down, thumbs together) in front of him or her. Then pull your hands apart to form dry land for the Miriam and Moses puppets to walk across. Encourage the kids to tell the story in their own words. Have one pair perform the puppet show, one pair narrate the story, and the third pair be the audience. Let the pairs take a turn in each role.

The Mountain
Blocks and Construction

To Do and To Notice—*Use blocks to construct Mount Sinai and remember the Ten Commandments Moses received there.*

As the children work, you can ask them these questions:
- **Who makes rules for you?**
- **How do rules help people?**
- **Why do you think God wants us to have rules?**

What? You'll need large cardboard or wooden blocks, a brown towel or sheet, and ten pieces of gray construction paper with the corners of the top edges rounded to look like stone tablets.

Where? Use the block center, or choose a floor space where the children can spread out and build.

How? As you introduce this center, remind the children that Moses climbed a mountain and God talked to him there. God gave Moses the Ten Commandments (God's rules) to take back down the mountain to the people. Show children the tablets made from gray construction paper, and count each one. Encourage the kids build a mountain out of blocks, cover it with the brown towel, and hide the commandments under the fabric. Let the children take turns walking two fingers up the mountain, collecting all the commandment tablets without making any blocks fall, and counting the tablets. Let the kids hide the commandments again, and let another child have a turn. If any of the blocks fall, all the children can help with the rebuilding.

Snake or Stick?
Small Motor Skills

To Do and To Notice—*Construct and put together a snake puzzle to remember that God demonstrated his power by changing Aaron's walking stick into a snake.*

As the children work, you can ask them these questions:
- **What do you think the king thought when Aaron's stick changed into a snake?**
- **How have you seen God's power?**
- **Moses was trying to tell the king about God when the stick turned into a snake. Who could you tell about God?**

What? You'll need photocopies of the puzzle pattern found on page 37 (you may want to enlarge the copies), crayons, sandwich-size resealable bags, and scissors.

Where? Set up a table and four to six chairs. Place a photocopy of the puzzle at each workspace, and make the rest of the supplies accessible each child.

How? Before class, color one of the photocopies and create a model. Allow the preschoolers to color their snake puzzle pictures and to cut out only the outline. Then let the children cut out the individual pieces, choosing which lines to cut on. Younger children may need help cutting. Have the children attempt to put the puzzles together from both the front and the back sides. Let them exchange puzzles for an extra challenge. Have each child keep his or her pieces in a resealable bag.

Snake or Stick?

Permission to photocopy this handout from *Wiggly, Giggly Bible Learning Centers for Preschoolers* granted for local church use.
Copyright © Group Publishing, Inc., P.O. Box 481, Loveland, CO 80539.

Joshua Trusts the Lord
Numbers 13:1–14:9

Joshua was known for his deep trust in the Lord. He was chosen by God to complete Moses' work, leading the Israelites into the Promised Land. Although others said there were too many obstacles to overcome, Joshua was brave and believed God would safely lead them.

After the story, these centers will help your children recognize Joshua's amazing trust in God. Kids will learn that they, too, can depend on God's mighty power.

Honey Art
Arts and Crafts

To Do and To Notice—*Use honey to create pictures and imagine what the Promised Land might have looked like to Joshua and Caleb when they saw it for the first time.*

As the children work, you can ask them these questions:
- **How do you think Joshua felt when he saw the Promised Land?**
- **What do you think the Promised Land looked like?**
- **What do you think it was like to live in a land flowing with milk and honey?**

What? You'll need construction paper, small bowls of honey, cotton swabs, pieces of yarn, cotton balls, and Easter grass.

Where? Set up a table and four to six chairs. At each workspace, set a small bowl of honey, a cotton swab, and a sheet of construction paper. Set the other supplies where they are accessible to all the children.

How? Explain to children that the Promised Land was a very beautiful place, flowing with milk and honey. Explain that they will use the honey as their glue to apply the items to their pictures. To do this they will dip the cotton swab in honey and touch it to the item they want to apply to the paper. Allow children to use their imagination to create pictures of what the Promised Land may have looked like.

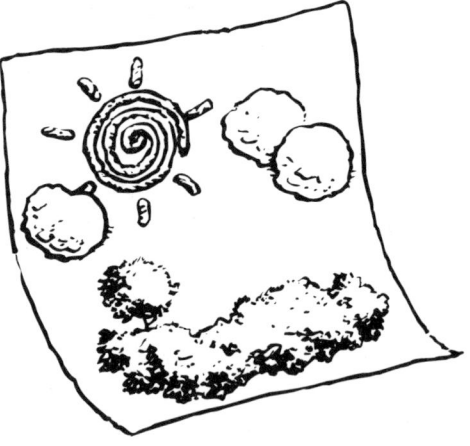

Promised Land Puppets
Storytelling

To Do and To Notice—*Make spoon puppets and use them to review the story of Joshua and Caleb entering the Promised Land.*

As the children work, you can ask them these questions:
- **What did Joshua and Caleb see when they entered the Promised Land?**
- **How would you have felt if you had seen giants?**
- **What would you have told Moses if you had been Joshua or Caleb?**

What? You'll need wooden or plastic spoons, yarn, glue, markers, and a bedsheet.

Where? Drape the sheet over a table to create both a work area and a puppet stage. Place all the materials where they are easily accessible to each child.

How? Have each child choose a character from the story of Joshua. Children might choose to be Joshua, Caleb, one of the other spies, or a giant from the land of Canaan. To make the puppet, they can glue yarn to the top of a spoon and draw a face on the spoon head. After kids have made their puppets, have them clear the table and duck down behind it as they use their puppets to act out the story of Joshua in the Promised Land.

Giants in the Promised Land
Readiness

To Do and To Notice—*Sort objects to help children understand the difference between the giants and the spies.*

As children work you can ask them these questions:
- **What was the difference between Joshua and the people he found in the Promised Land?**
- **What do you think the giants in the Promised Land looked like?**
- **Would you have been afraid of the giants? Why or why not?**

What? You'll need a variety of objects that come in small and large sizes. For example, you might use a mini-marshmallow and a large marshmallow, a small and a large foam cup, a piece of mini-wheat cereal and a large shredded wheat biscuit, a tennis ball and a beach ball, and a desk calendar and a wall calendar. You'll also need a laundry basket to place all the items in and a blanket.

Where? Spread out the blanket on the floor. Place the laundry basket in the center of the blanket.

How? Have children take turns sorting the different objects into a "spy" pile and a "giant" pile based on whether the item is small or large. As children work, encourage them to describe the differences in the objects. The children can also put the large and small similar items together in pairs. When all the items are sorted, the children can work together to place the objects in a row from smallest to largest.

Joshua's Concentration Games

To Do and To Notice—*Match pictures to think about what Joshua found in the Promised Land.*

As children work, you can ask them these questions:
- **What does** [name of the picture] **have to do with the Bible story of Joshua?**
- **What did the spies think about** [name of picture]?
- **Do you think there were more good things or bad things in the Promised Land?**
- **Why do you think Joshua and Caleb were the only ones who wanted to live in the Promised Land?**

What? Make two copies of the handout on page 41, cut apart the pictures, and mount them on index cards.

Where? Allow the children to sit on the floor around the rows of picture cards.

How? Place the cards upside down in rows on the floor. Let the kids flip one card at a time trying to find two that match. Each child may take a turn, flipping two cards per turn. When a child finds a match, he or she gets another turn. Encourage children to watch the cards that their friends turn over so they will remember where the cards are.

Joshua's Concentration

Rahab Saves Lives
Joshua 2

Rahab acknowledged God as the one true God, and her brave actions saved the lives of Joshua's spies and her entire extended family. God was honored by her bravery and Rahab was given an honored place in the lineage of David. From Rahab's example, children can discover the power of God and the rewards of brave choices.

Tell Rahab's story, then use these centers to help your preschoolers explore the details of Rahab's life and to imagine what it might have been like for Rahab to act bravely.

A Special House
Blocks and Construction

To Do and To Notice—*Build a house within a wall to discover how Rahab's house was a perfect place for spies to hide.*

As the children work, you can ask them these questions:
- **Why do you think this kind of house would be a good place for spies to hide?**
- **How do you think Rahab felt about hiding the spies in her house?**
- **What would be fun about having a house that was part of a big, tall wall around the city?**

What? You'll need a set of blocks, Lincoln Log or Lego construction toys, and an enlarged photocopy of "Rahab's House" (p. 43).

Where? Choose an area of the room that has a smooth, flat surface large enough for several children to be building at the same time.

How? As you introduce the center, discuss the picture, pointing out that the house in the picture is actually a part of the wall. Tell the children to use the blocks or other building materials to build a house that is part of a wall. Suggest building the house into the top of the wall, the middle of the wall, or at the bottom of the wall.

Around the Corner
Have children place the copy of the "Rahab's House" handout on a table or on the floor and fill in the outlines with blocks.

Rahab's House

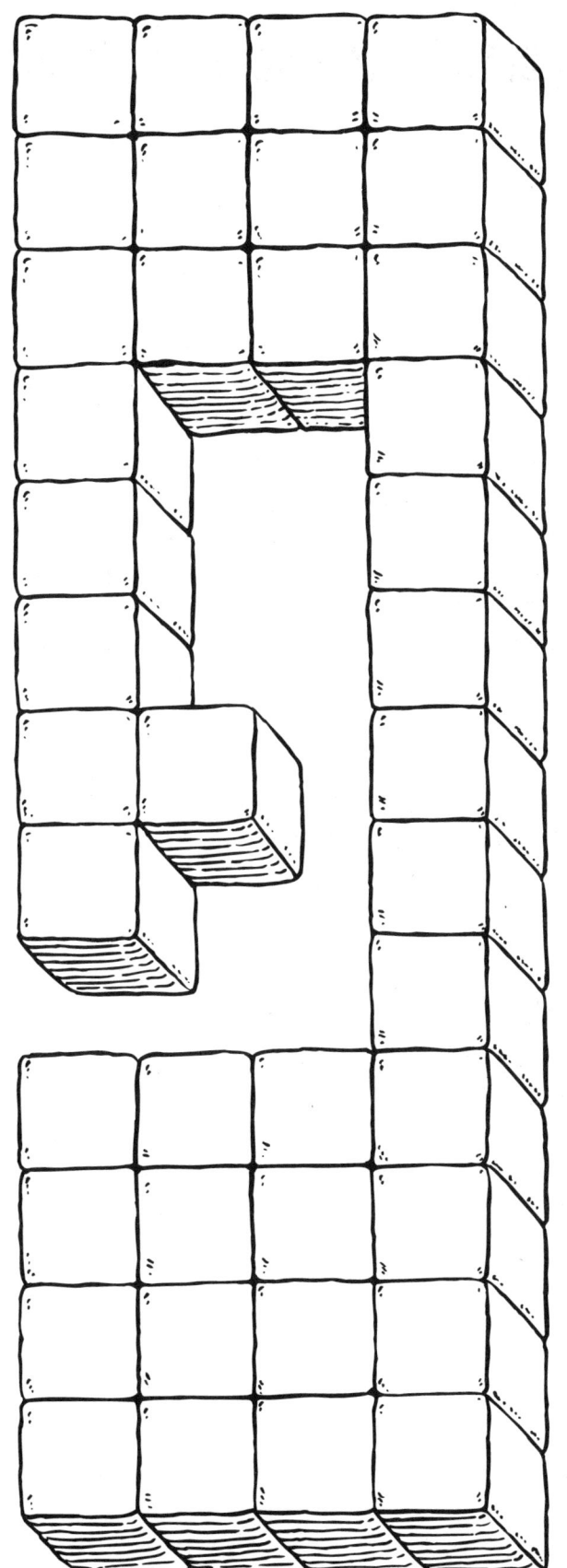

Where Are the Spies?
Dramatic and Imaginative Play

To Do and To Notice—*Pretend to be Rahab and try to hide toy spies on the roof under the straw.*

As the children work, you can ask them these questions:
- **What problems do you think Rahab might have had trying to hide the spies?**
- **How do you think Rahab felt when the soldiers came looking for the spies?**
- **Tell about a time you had to do a big job as Rahab did.**
- **How can God help us when we have a hard job to do?**

What? You'll need a box with a flat top, decorated to look like a Bible-times house (cut out several doors or windows so that the children can reach inside the box); several small play people; and a basket full of uncooked spaghetti or Easter grass in a neutral color.

Where? Choose an area of the room where you can place the Bible-times house so it is accessible from all sides and where cleanup will be easy.

How? As you introduce the center, show the children that the top of the house is flat—a perfect place for the spies to hide. Explain that Rahab hid the spies on the roof of her house by covering them with flax, which was a little like the material you've placed in the basket. Show the children how to cover the play people with the materials you've supplied. Have each child work with a partner, taking turns pretending to be Rahab (who hides the play people) and a soldier (who searches for the hidden spies). Encourage the children to play with the toy people outside, inside, and on top of the box house, imagining what might have happened before, during, and after Rahab hid the spies.

Around the Corner
Fill a wading pool with shredded paper, and let children take turns burying each other.

Rahab's Window
Arts and Crafts

To Do and To Notice—*Using precut shapes and yarn, create a picture of Rahab at her window.*

As the children work, you can ask them these questions:
- **Why was the red rope a good sign to tell the spies and their army to keep Rahab safe?**

- **How do you think Rahab felt when the spies told her to put the rope in her window?**

What? For each child, you'll need a 9x12-inch sheet of blue construction paper and a glue stick. Also set out 1-inch squares of brown construction paper (for each child, cut one sheet of brown paper into squares); 4-inch long pieces of red yarn; and 1-inch circles cut from beige construction paper, with a smiling face drawn on each one.

Where? Set up a table and four to six chairs. Place a piece of blue paper and a glue stick at each workspace. Place the other supplies so that they are accessible to each child. Display a model like the picture here.

How? Explain to the children that they will be making a picture of a wall, a window with a red rope hanging out of it, and a face in the window. Remind them that the red rope told the Israelite soldiers to protect the people in Rahab's house. Show them how to use a glue stick to put a small amount of glue on a large sheet of paper and then put a brown square on the glue. Allow children lots of freedom in designing this mosaiclike picture.

Rahab's Ropes
Small Motor Skills

To Do and To Notice—*Create red ropes with modeling dough to remind children of the rope that hung from Rahab's window.*

As the children work, you can ask them these questions:
- **How did the rope keep Rahab safe?**
- **How do you think Rahab and her family felt when the army did not harm them?**
- **Who or what keeps you safe?**

What? You'll need enough red modeling dough for each child at the center to have a fist-sized lump. Use commercial modeling dough or make your own from the recipe on page 108.

Where? Set up a table and four to six chairs. Put a plastic place mat at each workspace, and put the modeling dough where every child can reach it.

How? As you introduce the center, remind the children that after Rahab saved the spies, she hung a red rope from her window as a sign to the army of the Israelites to keep her safe. Show the children how to form ropes by rolling a small piece of dough on the table with their hands. They can make two ropes and twist them together to make a more realistic rope. Encourage kids to experiment with short ropes, long ropes, thick ropes, thin ropes, and ropes they can make together.

Wise and Mighty Deborah

Judges 4–5

Deborah was the only woman God appointed as judge over the children of Israel. She is remembered because she listened to and trusted God's words that Israel would defeat the king of Canaan, who held Israel in slavery. On the day of the battle, Deborah led the children of Israel to victory.

After hearing about Deborah, your preschoolers can participate in these centers to learn that many people came to ask her for help and wise advice. Deborah's example of worship and praise for everything God had done for her people can remind children that the power of even the wise and mighty comes from God.

The Deborah Palm
Listening and Music

To Do and To Notice—*Listen and follow directions to remember how Deborah obeyed God.*

As the children work, you can ask them these questions:
- **Why do you think God made Deborah wise?**
- **What are some special things about you?**
- **How do you think listening to your parents and teachers can make you wise?**

What? You'll need a tape recorder, a cassette tape, an umbrella, and a hat stand or upside-down chair. Before class, record the following song to the tune of "Frère Jacques":

Where is Deborah? Where is Deborah?
There she is! There she is!
She's under a big palm tree, under a big palm tree.
Helping God! Helping God!

Where is Deborah? Where is Deborah?
There she is! There she is!
She tells God's people wise things, tells God's people wise things.
Follow God! Follow God!

Then record the following instructions for the children to complete after listening to the song.
- **Give a hug to someone sitting or standing next to you.**
- **Clap your hands three times.**
- **Stamp your feet four times.**

Where? Choose an area that is away from quiet activities. Place a hat stand in the center of the area. Open the umbrella, and slip the handle through the top of the hat stand to form a "palm tree." Place the tape recorder and the tape you recorded where they are accessible to the children.

How? As you introduce the center, show the children how to use the tape recorder, including how to rewind the tape. Remind them that Deborah helped God's people know what to do when they came to talk to her under a palm tree. Encourage the children to sit under the "Deborah Palm." Direct them to listen to the Deborah song on the tape and to follow the directions they hear. Suggest that the children pretend to be Deborah sitting under the palm tree as people come by for help and advice. After the children have listened to the tape several times, encourage them to take turns making up directions the others can follow.

Banner Praise
Prayer and Worship

To Do and To Notice—*Take turns leading worship as Deborah led Israel's victory celebration.*

As the children work, you can ask them these questions:
- **What great things do you remember God doing?**
- **How do you feel when God helps you with something that is hard to do?**
- **How do you think God feels when his people worship as Deborah or you did?**

What? You'll need a flat bedsheet, strong tape, a CD or tape of praise music and a CD or tape player, six sticks for stirring paint (available at paint or hardware stores), six pieces of felt (approximately 6x6-inch squares), and a stapler.

Where? Choose a corner of the room with plenty of space where the children can sing and worship without disturbing other kids. Tape a sheet across the corner near the ceiling to form a center area that resembles a worship tent. Staple each square of felt to a paint stick to create a mini-banner, and put the banners inside the worship tent. Place the music player on the floor so children can reach it.

How? As you introduce the center, remind the children that after Israel's victory Deborah led the people in praise. Select one child to be Deborah, and let that child stand facing the other kids. Give each child a paint stick with felt attached to it, and turn on the music. The child playing Deborah can move the banner in any way he or she wishes. The rest of the children should try to copy the motions with their own banners. Encourage the children to worship God from their hearts by thanking God for all he does for them. Let the children take turns leading the others, switching leaders as the music stops and starts.

Block Battle
Blocks and Construction

To Do and To Notice—*Build Mount Tabor, the place where Barak's men waited for Deborah to tell them to go and fight the battle.*

As the children work, you can ask them these questions:
- **How do you think Barak felt when Deborah told him to go down the mountain and fight?**
- **Deborah believed God would help the men win the battle. Why do you think Deborah believed God?**
- **God wants to be your helper. What would you like God to help you do?**

What? You'll need a brown towel, small and large cardboard or wooden blocks, plastic play figures, and masking tape.

Where? Set the blocks and towel in an area with lots of open floor space. Use masking tape to secure the plastic play figures to small blocks so that they can easily be manipulated.

How? As you introduce this center, say: **Barak waited at Mount Tabor for Deborah to tell him when he and his men could go down the mountain to fight the enemy. Deborah believed God would help them win the battle.** Direct children to build a mountain with the blocks and to cover the blocks with a brown towel to make the structure look like a mountain. Allow the children to place the play figures around the mountain and at the top. Tell the children to pretend to be Barak and his soldiers. Let one child pretend to be Deborah and say to the soldiers, "Go down from the mountain and fight the battle." The rest of the children should immediately move the soldiers down the mountain. Let the children build the mountain and act out the story several times.

Job Badges
Arts and Crafts

To Do and To Notice—*Choose jobs to do in class or at home and make badges telling others about the jobs.*

As the children work, you can ask them these questions:
- **God gave Deborah the job of being a judge and helping people solve problems. Do you know someone who helps people solve problems?**
- **What do you think helped Deborah make wise decisions?**
- **Who can help you do your jobs well?**

What? You'll need 3-inch shapes cut from poster board (squares, stars, circles, or triangles), aluminum foil (cut into pieces large enough to cover the poster-board shapes), double-stick tape, and spring-type clothespins. You'll also need enough photocopies of the "Special Jobs Chart" handout (p. 51) to give one to each child in the class. Fill in the spaces labeled "Other" with jobs unique to your class.

Where? Set up a table and four to six chairs. At each workspace, put one piece of foil and a spring-type clothespin with a line of double-stick tape on one side.

How? As you introduce the center, explain that God gave Deborah a special job to do. Tell children that they each have special jobs, too. Help the children think of some jobs such as helper, hugger, and smiler. The children may wish to name more specific classroom jobs such as plant waterer, crayon monitor, and song leader.

Show the children how to cover their poster-board shapes with foil, molding the foil around the edges. When children have finished this step, they can stick the shape to the double-stick tape on the clothespin. Have children each look at the "Special Jobs Chart" handout and clip their badges to the jobs they would like to do.

Around the Corner
You can let the children decorate their foil-covered shapes with glitter glue or puffy paint for extra pizazz!

Special Jobs Chart

Permission to photocopy this chart from *Wiggly, Giggly Bible Learning Centers for Preschoolers* granted for local church use.
Copyright © Group Publishing, Inc., P.O. Box 481, Loveland, CO 80539.

Trusting Gideon
Judges 6–7

God made Gideon a hero in the sight of the children of Israel and gave him victory over the Midianites in the Promised Land of Canaan. Gideon repeatedly asked God to prove himself, and God patiently responded, building Gideon's trust. Gideon went into battle with only three hundred men and no weapons. Because of God's promise, Gideon and his men took over the camp from the Midianites. From that day on, Gideon was a hero to the children of Israel.

Tell children the story, then use these centers to help your preschoolers learn about Gideon's role and relationship with God. Your children can be faith heroes, too, as they learn to trust God with their lives.

Fleece Squeezing
Wet and Dry

To Do and To Notice—*Squeeze water from different materials and remember that Gideon's fleece helped him to trust God.*

As the children work, you can ask them these questions:
- **What did Gideon learn about God from the wet fleece?**
- **Why do you think Gideon asked God for a dry fleece?**
- **What helps you to trust God?**

What? You'll need one dishpan half-filled with water; one empty dishpan; a bath towel; two sponges; and several sturdy, absorbent cloths (including fleece, if available).

Where? Place the dishpan of water and the empty dishpan on a table, and put the bath towel between them. Leave plenty of room around the table for the children to circulate. Place the pieces of cloth and sponges on the table near the dishpans. You may also want to place a plastic tablecloth under the table.

How? As you introduce this center, remind children that Gideon wanted to make sure that God was asking him to lead his people, so Gideon asked God to make a sheepskin wet while leaving the ground around it dry. In the morning, Gideon squeezed a whole bowl full of water from the sheepskin. The children's task in this center will be to try to move the water from one dishpan to the other without wetting the table around it. Show children how to use the sponges and pieces of cloth to absorb water from the dishpan, letting some of the water drip back into the dishpan so the table doesn't get wet. Then show kids how to wring the rest of the water into the empty dishpan. Help the children to recognize the difficulty of filling the empty dishpan without getting the table or towel wet, and to understand that God's act was a true miracle.

Marching Boots
Home and Life Skills

To Do and To Notice—*Practice lacing and tying skills and remember that God led Gideon's army to victory.*

As the children work, you can ask them these questions:
- **What do boots do for soldiers?**
- **How was Gideon's army protected?**
- **Who was Gideon's leader? Who is your leader?**

What? You'll need four to six pairs of men's unlaced army or hunting boots; four to six large, clean pairs of socks; and clean boot laces for each pair of boots.

Where? Choose an area of the room with open floor space where children can spread out and march freely.

How? Let the children explore the different boots. Start lacing the boots, and then let the children work on finishing the job. Direct them to put on the big socks and boots and march as the soldiers of Gideon's army may have marched. Encourage children to help one another and to trade boots as they play.

Around the Corner

Instead of using only large boots and socks, provide boots and socks of different sizes and have the children match the boots to the proper socks.

Trusting Tunnel
Dramatic and Imaginative Play

To Do and To Notice—*Pretend to be Gideon and his army carrying torches in empty jars.*

As the children work, you can ask them these questions:
- **Gideon may have been afraid to fight without a big army. When have you been afraid?**
- **What do you do when you're afraid?**
- **How do you think Gideon's soldiers felt when they got to the enemy camp? after they overtook the enemy?**

What? You'll need four to six two-liter plastic bottles, four to six mini-flashlights, eight child-size chairs, and a large blanket.

Where? Choose a large, open area. Put the chairs in two parallel lines, and cover them with the blanket to make a dark tunnel. Place the head of each flashlight inside the neck of a plastic bottle so the light will shine through the bottle. (Cut the necks off the bottles if the flashlights are too large to fit.)

How? As you introduce the center, remind the children that Gideon's army went into the enemy camp at night, and that the soldiers carried empty jars with torches. Direct one child to pretend to be Gideon. He or she will stand at the end of the tunnel and call to a person at the other end with the words, "Believe God, [child's name]!" The person whose name is called will then carry the lighted flashlight and sneak quietly through the tunnel just as Gideon's army sneaked over to the enemy's camp. As each child comes out of the tunnel, he or she will call out, "For the Lord and for Gideon!" Let the children take turns pretending to be Gideon.

Gideon's Trumpets
Listening and Music

To Do and To Notice—*Make a trumpet as a reminder of how Gideon's soldiers won the battle.*

As the children work, you can ask them these questions:
- **Why do you think God told Gideon's soldiers to blow their horns?**
- **How would you feel about sneaking around an enemy's camp at night?**
- **What did Gideon's soldiers learn about following God's plan?**
- **What have you learned about following God?**

What? You'll need a cardboard paper towel tube for each child, markers or stickers for decorating, wax paper, and rubber bands.

Where? Set up a table and four to six chairs. At each workspace, place one cardboard tube with several holes punched along the side, one 6x6-inch piece of wax paper, and a rubber band. Place the decorating items where they are accessible to each child.

How? Remind the children that the soldiers in Gideon's army used trumpets to scare their enemies. Show the children how to put the end of a tube on the wax paper, bring the paper up around the sides of the tubes, and secure the wax paper with a rubber band. Children may need help with the last step. Let the children decorate the tubes with markers or stickers. When kids have finished, encourage them to explore the sounds they can make with their trumpets. Encourage the children to work in pairs and to try to make the sounds of their trumpets match so that they sound like one big trumpet instead of two little ones.

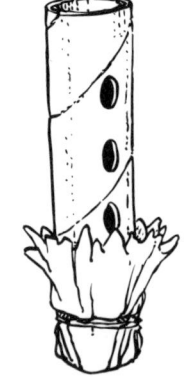

Strong, Brave Samson
Judges 13–16

Samson is a favorite Bible character among preschoolers. According to biblical accounts, he was strong and very brave. Samson didn't seem to be afraid of anything, even death. His weaknesses were his love for Delilah and his uncontrollable temper. It's important that the children understand that Samson was a mighty man of God only when he put God first in his life. It was only after Samson realized this that God forgave him and restored his strength so that Samson could finish the work God had planned.

First tell the story of Samson. Then use these centers to help preschoolers remember Samson's long hair and superhuman strength. Most important, help them understand that this strong man needed God just as they do.

Samson's Hair
Dramatic and Imaginative Play

To Do and To Notice—*Pretend to comb long hair like Samson's and pull apart licorice strings to show that God gave Samson his strength.*

As the children work, you can ask them these questions:
- **What do you think Samson liked about having long hair?**
- **What would you like about having long hair like Samson's?**
- **Samson's hair reminded him of a promise to God. What promises have you made to God?**

What? You'll need hairbrushes, longhaired dolls, red string licorice, and a new comb for each child (optional).

Where? Choose an open area where the children have space to move around.

How? Remind children that Samson's long hair was the secret to his strength, and that by keeping his hair long, he was keeping a promise to God. Have the children brush the dolls' hair. If you've provided fresh combs, have children pretend their hair is extra long as they comb their own hair. To demonstrate that Samson was strong enough to split ropes, have children use the dolls' hands to pull apart the strings of licorice.

Around the Corner
Acquire several wigs, and allow children to try them on. As children wear the wigs, allow other kids to comb or brush the hair.

Lion's Bones

Science and Nature

To Do and To Notice—*Find "lion" bones and bees by digging in the sand to remember that God helped Samson wrestle a lion.*

As the children work, you can ask them these questions:
- **What do you think it would be like to wrestle a lion as Samson did?**
- **How do you think Samson beat the big lion?**
- **What do you think God can do to help you?**

What? You'll need chicken or turkey bones that have been boiled and cleaned and have no sharp edges. (You can soak the cleaned bones in two parts water and one part bleach for two to four minutes for whitening.) You'll also need a sand table or tub filled with sand, plastic bees, and small shovels or spoons. (If you are unable to find plastic bees, you can laminate pictures of bees from a nature magazine or another source.)

Where? Choose an area of the room where the children can play in the sand without worrying about sand getting on the floor. Bury the bones and the bees in the sandbox.

How? Encourage the children to pretend to be Samson as he walked down the road, killed the lion, and later found the bees and honey among the lion's bones. Direct children to dig in the sand to find the bones and the bees.

Around the Corner

Provide honey graham crackers or the lions from a box of animal crackers, and let kids eat a cracker with honey each time they dig up a bee.

Let's Eat

Home and Life Skills

To Do and To Notice—*Sort pictures of food into categories based on whether the foods will help children grow strong.*

As the children work, you can ask them these questions:
- **What foods do you like to eat?**
- **How do you feel when you eat too much candy or drink too much pop?**
- **God told Samson to eat only those foods that were good for his body. What kind of foods do you think God wants us to eat?**

What? You'll need two shoeboxes with a slit cut into the top of each. Label one box with pictures of desserts and the other with pictures of fruits or vegetables. You'll also need magazines with lots of pictures of food.

Where? Do this activity in the area of the room that has already been designated as a home center. If you don't have a home center, choose an open area where the children will have plenty of room to work. Set out the magazines, and put the boxes in the center of the area.

How? As you introduce the center, remind children that God wanted Samson to eat healthy foods and that eating good foods was part of what made Samson strong. Show children the boxes, and tell them that the box labeled with the desserts means "eat only a little of these foods." Tell them that the box labeled with the fruit or vegetable pictures means "eat a lot of these healthy foods." Have the children look through the magazines to find pictures of food, and let them tear out the pictures. Have them decide if the foods would help them grow strong or not. Then they can place the pictures in the appropriate boxes.

Lion Target
Games

To Do and To Notice—*Pretend to be Samson conquering a lion by throwing beanbags at a lion target.*

As the children work, you can ask them these questions:
- **If God helped Samson conquer a lion, what can God help you do?**
- **How can you help others?**

What? You'll need an enlarged photocopy of the lion target (p. 58) mounted on a piece of poster board, several beanbags, and tape.

Where? Choose an area of the room where the lion target can be taped on the wall and where the children have room to throw. Place a piece of masking tape on the floor to identify where the children will stand to throw the beanbags.

How? Encourage the children to pretend to be Samson conquering the lion. One at a time have kids stand on the tape line, carefully sight the lion, and throw the beanbags. Let the children take turns and choose for themselves when they are ready to take a step backward for an extra challenge.

Lion Target

Ruth Loves Her Family Unselfishly
Ruth 1–4

Ruth demonstrated unconditional, selfless love for her mother-in-law, Naomi. Ruth followed Naomi back to Naomi's own country and she provided for her mother-in-law's needs.

After you've told the story, use these centers to help children explore the depth of Ruth's devotion to Naomi. Preschoolers will learn that they, too, can care for their families.

Gleaning Grain — Small Motor Skills

To Do and To Notice—*Experience a bit of the tedium involved in gleaning small bits of grain and learn that Ruth worked hard to help Naomi.*

As the children work, you can ask them these questions:
- **Do you enjoy this activity? Is it fun?**
- **Gathering a real bushel of grain would take many hours. How do you think you would feel after doing this for hours?**
- **How do you think Naomi felt when Ruth brought home grain for them to eat?**

What? You'll need a blanket, one three-ounce paper cup, a roasting pan, two pounds of cornmeal, and a cup of rice.

Where? Lay the blanket on the floor. Fill the roasting pan with the cornmeal and rice, and place it in the center of the blanket. Set the paper cup to the side.

How? Explain to the children that they will be gleaning grain just as Ruth did for Naomi. Have them all stand around the roasting pan. Ask them to work together to fill the cup with rice, one grain at a time. Tell the children not to put any of the rice into their mouths since it is uncooked.

Around the Corner
For a fun challenge, set a timer for three minutes. Ask the children to see if they can fill the "bushel" before the timer goes off. But remind them to be careful—if someone knocks over the cup they'll have to start all over again!

We're Thankful for Food
Home and Life Skills

> **To Do and To Notice**—*Create and pretend to serve foods made of modeling dough.*

As the children work, you can ask them these questions:
- **What kinds of food do you like?**
- **How do you like to eat this food?** (Modify this question as necessary. For example, you could ask, "What do you like to put on your hot dog?")
- **How do you think Naomi felt when Ruth brought food for her to eat?**
- **What do you think Naomi might have said to Ruth after Ruth brought her the food?**

What? You'll need several different colors of modeling dough (make your own from the recipe on page 108) and tools for sculpting the dough.

Where? Set up a table and four to six chairs. Put the modeling dough on the table where it is accessible to all the children.

How? Remind the children that Ruth gathered grain for Naomi to cook. They might have eaten the grain as cereal, as bread, or in soup. Tell the children to use the modeling dough to make foods for which they feel thankful. Allow them lots of leeway in how they do this—the food doesn't have to look realistic! Encourage them to pretend to serve others these yummy snacks and to practice good manners by saying "please" and "thank you."

Stick With Me
Games

> **To Do and To Notice**—*Complete an obstacle course with a partner to discover how it feels to stick with someone.*

As the children work, you can ask them these questions:
- **How did it feel to work with a partner?**
- **What problems did you have?**
- **Was it easier to work with a partner or by yourself?**
- **Do you think it would have been easier or harder for Ruth and Naomi to have been alone?**
- **Who do you stick by and help?**

What? You'll need to set up a short obstacle course using tables, chairs, and other classroom items. Tape paper arrows around the course to show the children how to proceed through the course. You'll also need a soft ball for every two children in the center.

Where? Choose a large, open area with plenty of room to construct an obstacle course.

How? As you introduce the center, proceed through the obstacle course yourself, pointing out which obstacles must be climbed over, crawled under, or walked around. Point out that the arrows help you find the route. Then ask a child to be your partner, and proceed through the course holding hands. Finally, show the children how to use the ball to keep you and your partner together. Decide together how the two of you will hold onto the ball as you proceed through the obstacle course. Tell the kids that neither partner can let go of the ball at any time. If they drop the ball, they should pick it up and start over. Each person will go through the course in the three ways you described. Children can choose different partners if time allows.

Ruth and Naomi
Science and Nature

To Do and To Notice—*Use paper dolls to explore the pull of magnetism.*

As the children work, you can ask them these questions:
- **Why did Ruth stay with Naomi?**
- **How do you think Naomi felt about Ruth?**
- **Ruth and Naomi weren't held together with magnets or tape. What did hold them together?**
- **Ruth helped Naomi through some hard times. How can you help people you love?**

What? You'll need photocopies of the Ruth and Naomi figures on page 62; scissors; self-adhesive magnet strips; double-stick tape; paper clips; and various metal and nonmetal items such as cookie sheets, silverware, plastic toys, large metal washers, and jar lids. Before class, cut out several sets of the Ruth and Naomi figures. Put a magnet strip on the back of each Ruth figure. Use double-stick tape to attach a paper clip to the back of each Naomi figure.

Where? Place the supplies around a small table. Allow plenty of room for children to circulate. If you have a metal cabinet or other metal object in the room, you may want to set up this center near it.

How? As you introduce the center, show children the Ruth and Naomi figures. Let children experiment with the figures. Ask them how close together the two figures have to be before they stick to each other. Ask children if the figures would stick together if a hand was placed between them. Ask what would happen if two Ruth figures or two Naomi figures faced each other. Encourage the children to try to stick the figures to other objects on the table. Let kids share their findings with other children in the center.

Around the Corner
Suggest that children see what objects the magnet ("Ruth") will stick to in the room. Encourage children to guess what objects the magnet will stick to, and then have them test their hypotheses!

Ruth and Naomi

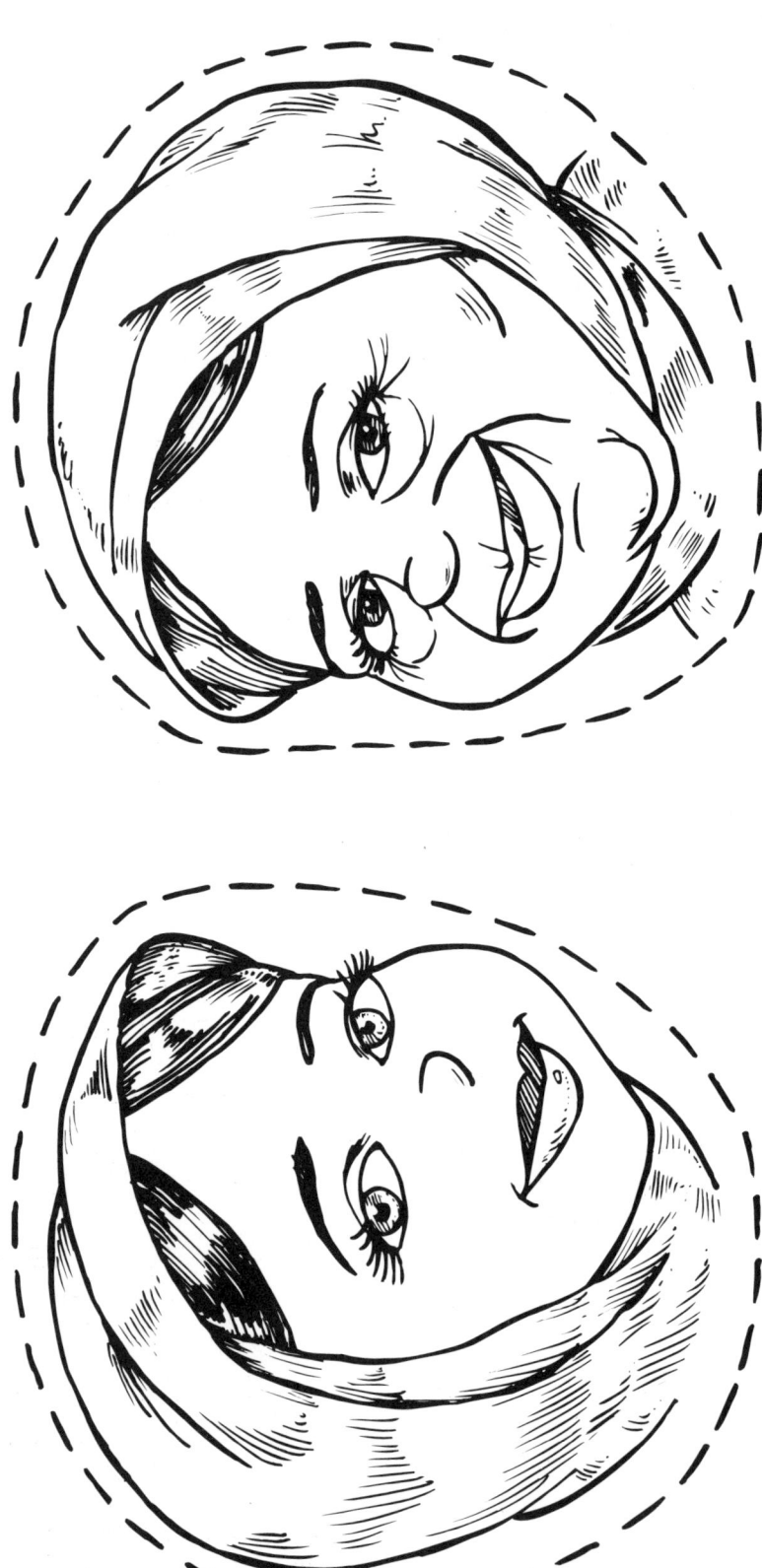

Hannah Has Great Faith
1 Samuel 1:1–2:21

Hannah had great faith in the Lord and a strong desire to have a child. When God granted her request for a child, Hannah dedicated the child to God and took him to the temple to live. Her faith was further rewarded when God gave her additional children to love.

After the children have heard the story, these centers will provide many ways for preschoolers to explore and experience the great faith Hannah had in the Lord and the love Hannah had for her son Samuel. Your children can learn that God will honor their faithfulness, too.

A Gift for Samuel
Arts and Crafts

To Do and To Notice—*Weave a "blanket" using construction paper to remember Hannah's love for her son as he served the Lord.*

As the children work, you can ask them these questions:
- **How long do you think it took each year for Hannah to weave a robe for her son?**
- **Why do you think Hannah wanted to take Samuel a present each time she went to see him?**
- **What kind of presents can you give to show people how much you love them?**
- **What can you do to show God that you love him?**

What? You'll need 9x12-inch sheets of construction paper with slits cut every two inches across the middle of the page with a 1-inch solid border around each side. You'll also need glue sticks and 2x9-inch strips of paper in various colors.

Around the Corner

To simplify this project for the children, use double-stick tape to attach the weaving strips to the prepared sheets of paper before the children start to work.

Where? Set up a low table and four to six chairs. Put a sheet of the prepared construction paper and a glue stick at each workspace. Put the strips where they are easily accessible to each child.

How? As you introduce this center, remind the children that even though Hannah allowed Samuel to live in the temple, she continued to show her love for him. Each year she made him new clothes. Show the children how to weave the cut strips into the prepared sheet of construction paper to make a "blanket," similar to the way Hannah might have made a robe for Samuel. Show the children how to apply a little glue to the end of each paper strip and secure the strip to the sheet of paper before they begin to weave. Emphasize the words "over" and "under" as you demonstrate. Put the model you've created at the center for children to refer to.

Rock-a-Bye Samuel
Home and Life Skills

> **To Do and To Notice**—*Experience the needs of a new baby and appreciate the beauty of soft music by pretending to rock babies to sleep while listening to music.*

As the children work, you can ask them these questions:
- **What do you like to do just before going to sleep at night?**
- **Who tucks you into bed at your house?**
- **What does that person do to show you that he or she loves you?**
- **How do you think Hannah helped baby Samuel go to sleep at night?**

What? You'll need a CD player and CDs with lullabies, classical music, or soft, quiet hymns; small rocking chairs or pillows; and several baby dolls.

Where? Place the chairs or pillows and the dolls in an area of the room away from other centers to provide a quiet, restful atmosphere. Plug in the music player nearby.

How? As you introduce the center, explain to the children that moms and dads often hold or rock a baby to comfort, feed, or help the baby to sleep. We know that Hannah sang a song of praise to God, and she may have sung to baby Samuel, too. Show the children how to use the music player, and encourage them to listen quietly to the music and rock a "baby" to sleep. Encourage kids to sing and talk to the babies as they play.

Busy Babies
Home and Life Skills

To Do and To Notice—*Make a story mural to show how grown-ups love and care for babies.*

As the children work, you can ask them these questions:
- **What is the grown-up doing with the baby?**
- **Which of these things do you think Hannah did with baby Samuel?**
- **How does your mommy or daddy show you that she or he cares for you and loves you?**
- **How can you tell that God cares for you and loves you?**

What? You'll need a large piece of butcher paper, tape, glue sticks, family magazines, and child-safe scissors (optional).

Where? Choose an area with blank wall space. Tape the butcher paper to the wall so that the bottom edge is along the floor. Put the magazines, scissors, and glue sticks near the mural.

How? Explain to the children that parents or caregivers have many ways of showing their children that they love them. Encourage kids to look through the magazines to find pictures of people caring for babies. Suggest that the children quietly discuss with a partner what is happening in each picture or take turns making up a story about each picture. Have each child choose a favorite picture to cut or tear out and glue to the mural.

Around the Corner
A helper could write each child's dictated caption under the picture the child selects.

Hannah Prays
Prayer and Worship

To Do and To Notice—*Praise God for his blessings as Hannah did.*

As the children work, you can ask them these questions:
- **What can you pray to God about?**
- **How do you think Hannah felt when her prayers were answered?**
- **What do you think Hannah said to God when he answered her prayers?**

What? You'll need pictures of things that remind children of the good things in their lives (use magazine pictures or computer clip art), a shoebox, and a hand-held mirror.

Where? Put the pictures inside the shoebox. Place the shoebox on the floor with enough surrounding area to seat four to six children.

How? As you introduce the center, remind the children that Hannah used her lips, but not her voice, to pray for a son. Let the children practice mouthing words you ask them to imitate. Have one child take a picture from the box without looking, and tell him or her to place the picture face up on the floor. Pass the mirror around and invite children each to mouth a prayer about the person or thing the picture reminds them of. For example, if the picture is of a puppy, the prayer may be as simple as "Thank you, God, for my puppy." Or children may elaborate and pray for a neighbor's sick puppy, for the person who gave the child a puppy, or for homes for puppies that are living in animal shelters. Have the children pray as simply or in as much detail as they feel led to do. Let them look at their mouths in the mirror as they speak silently, and then pass the mirror to another child who is ready to pray. When all the children have finished praying about the first picture, another child may pull a picture from the box and repeat the process.

Samuel Hears the Voice of God
1 Samuel 3

Samuel, a young, impressionable boy, spent most of his early years assisting Eli, the high priest. One night Samuel heard a voice calling him. At first he thought it was Eli, but after three times Eli told Samuel to listen carefully because it was the Lord speaking to him. Preschoolers will be interested to know that even though Samuel was a young boy, he performed important tasks in the church and listened to and obeyed God.

After children have heard the story, these centers will provide many ways for preschoolers to discover truths about the story of Samuel. Help your children learn that they are not too young to listen to the voice and calling of God.

Ears to Hear
Science and Nature

To Do and To Notice—*Make megaphones to use in a game of listening.*

As the children work, you can ask them these questions:
- **What kinds of things do you like to hear?**
- **What did Samuel hear?**
- **How do you feel if someone doesn't listen to you?**

What? Set out a precut piece of tagboard for each child (see the example in the margin), markers or crayons, stickers, and tape.

Where? Set up a table and four to six chairs. Put a megaphone pattern at each workspace, and place the rest of the supplies where they are accessible to all the children.

How? Before class, make a megaphone following the margin example. Explain to children that Samuel learned to listen to God. Explain that the children are going to create devices that can be

67

used to help them hear better. These devices can also make their voices sound louder. Show kids the megaphone, and let several children either listen or speak through it. Encourage children to decorate the sheets of tagboard. Then they may and roll and tape them so that their megaphones look like the model you made. Let the kids use their megaphones to hear sounds more clearly, and encourage them to talk through the megaphones.

Sound Off
Listening and Music

To Do and To Notice—*Listen to noises and match them to their sources.*

As the children work, you can ask them these questions:
- **Was it easier to be the noisemaker or the listener?**
- **How did Samuel listen to God?**
- **How do you listen to God?**

What? You'll need a variety of items you can use to make unique sounds, such as a plastic soda bottle half-filled with water, a baby rattle, a plastic grocery bag, a paper bag, a bell, a pencil and sharpener, a bag of beans, an unopened package of cereal, and two spoons.

Where? Set up a table with three to five chairs on one side facing away from the table. Set all the sound items on the table.

How? Select one child to be the noisemaker and stand behind the table while the rest of the children sit in the chairs facing away from the table. Have the child choose one item and manipulate it to make a sound, and let the other kids try to determine what item made the sound. Let the children take turns being the noisemaker. Encourage the children to make unusual sounds with the items to try to confuse the listeners.

Service With a Smile
Home and Life Skills

To Do and To Notice—*Pretend to be Samuel and learn how he might have served in the church.*

As the children work, you can ask them these questions:
- **Was it hard to wash and dry all the dishes and put them away?**
- **What other jobs do you think Samuel did when he helped Eli?**
- **How could you be like Samuel and serve in the church?**
- **How can God help us when we have hard jobs to do?**

What? You'll need items from your classroom that can be cleaned in soapy water, a dishpan of soapy water, dishcloths, a dishpan of clear water, and towels.

Where? Set up this center in the home center area, or set up a table with the dishpans and other supplies on it, making sure there is plenty of space for the children to work around the table.

How? Remind the children that Samuel worked with Eli from the time he was their age. One of the things he probably did was clean up. Ask the children to find things that need cleaning in the home center, and have them wash and dry the items. Some children may wish to use the dishcloths to wipe surfaces around the center area. Encourage the kids to pretend that they are Samuel and to talk about serving God as they work.

It's Bedtime
Blocks and Construction

To Do and To Notice—*Use blocks to make beds for Eli and Samuel dolls to sleep in.*

As the children work, you can ask them these questions:
- **What kind of a bed do you have?**
- **Who else sleeps in your room?**
- **Do you ever wake up in the night? What do you do?**
- **How do you think Samuel felt when God woke him up in the night?**

What? You'll need large blocks, small blankets, dolls, and doll clothes.

Where? Choose an area of the room with plenty of floor space where there is room for several children to build beds with the blocks. Place all the other supplies in the area.

How? Remind the children that Samuel was asleep in bed when he heard the voice of God. Have children build doll beds using the blocks. Then children can make the beds using the blankets, get the dolls ready for bed, and tuck them in. Encourage the children to act out the details of the story as they play, whispering "Samuel," and having the dolls respond.

David Defeats Goliath
1 Samuel 17

When David fought the giant Goliath, God helped someone little do something big...and become a hero! This concept will delight children.

After telling the story, use these centers to help preschoolers learn about big and little and about how God helped David do great things. Help children discover that with God's help they, too, can accomplish big things.

Big and Little Footsteps
Listening and Music

To Do and To Notice—*Listen and re-create light and heavy footsteps to imagine what David's and Goliath's footsteps might have sounded like.*

As the children work, you can ask them these questions:
- **How do you think people felt when they heard Goliath's footsteps?**
- **How do you think people felt when they heard David's footsteps?**
- **What kinds of sounds do you enjoy making with your feet?**

What? You'll need a tape recorder and a cassette tape. Before class, record twenty seconds of light footsteps; ten seconds of silence; twenty seconds of heavy, pounding footsteps; ten seconds of silence; twenty seconds of jumping; ten seconds of silence; twenty seconds of shuffling; ten seconds of silence; and twenty seconds of toe tapping.

Where? Choose an area of the room with bare floor space (or set a piece of plywood on the floor). Set up a tape recorder with the sound effects tape you created so that it is accessible to the children.

How? As you introduce the center, show the children how to use the cassette recorder to play the tape you created before class. Ask them to listen to the footsteps on the tape, and then to try to imitate the sounds with their own feet. After the children have done the activity with the tape, have one child make a sound with his or her feet while the other children's eyes are closed. Then have the rest of the children imitate the example.

Around the Corner
Challenge the children to imitate the sound of the footsteps of various animals such as cats, mice, dinosaurs, ducks, ants, horses, and kangaroos.

David the Shepherd
Storytelling

To Do and To Notice—*Explore David's compassion and courage by acting out the story of David protecting his sheep from a lion and a bear.*

After the children act out the story, you can ask them these questions:
- **Was David a good shepherd? Why or why not?**
- **What do you think would be hard about being a shepherd?**
- **What do you think David might have been thinking when he saw the lion?**
- **How is God like a good shepherd caring for us?**

What? You'll need a sandbox or dishpan filled with about four inches of sand or salt; a copy of the David, lion, and bear figures on page 72, along with several copies of the sheep figure; craft sticks; and tape. You may wish to have some silk greenery or other plastic objects available to help you create the scene.

Where? Place the sandbox on a plastic tablecloth on the floor. Tape the David, lion, bear, and sheep figures to the craft sticks, and place them beside the sandbox.

How? Explain to the children that they can use stick figures to act out the story of David protecting his sheep from a lion and a bear. Show children how to bury the end of the sticks in the sand or salt so that the figures stand up. Remind preschoolers of the general sequence of the story, then let the children choose how to use the sandbox and surrounding area to act out the story. Encourage them to have fun making the sounds of the animals. The children can take turns being David and the different animals as they repeat the action several times.

Footprints
Arts and Crafts

To Do and To Notice—*Make little and big "footprints" to understand the difference between David's and Goliath's footprints.*

As the children work, you can ask them these questions:
- **Who has the biggest footprints in your family? the smallest?**
- **Which is usually stronger: big or little?**
- **Why was what David did to Goliath so amazing?**

What? You'll need a 9x12-inch piece of construction paper for each child, newsprint, washable paint, a sponge paintbrush, a damp sponge, a paper plate, and damp paper towels.

David the Shepherd

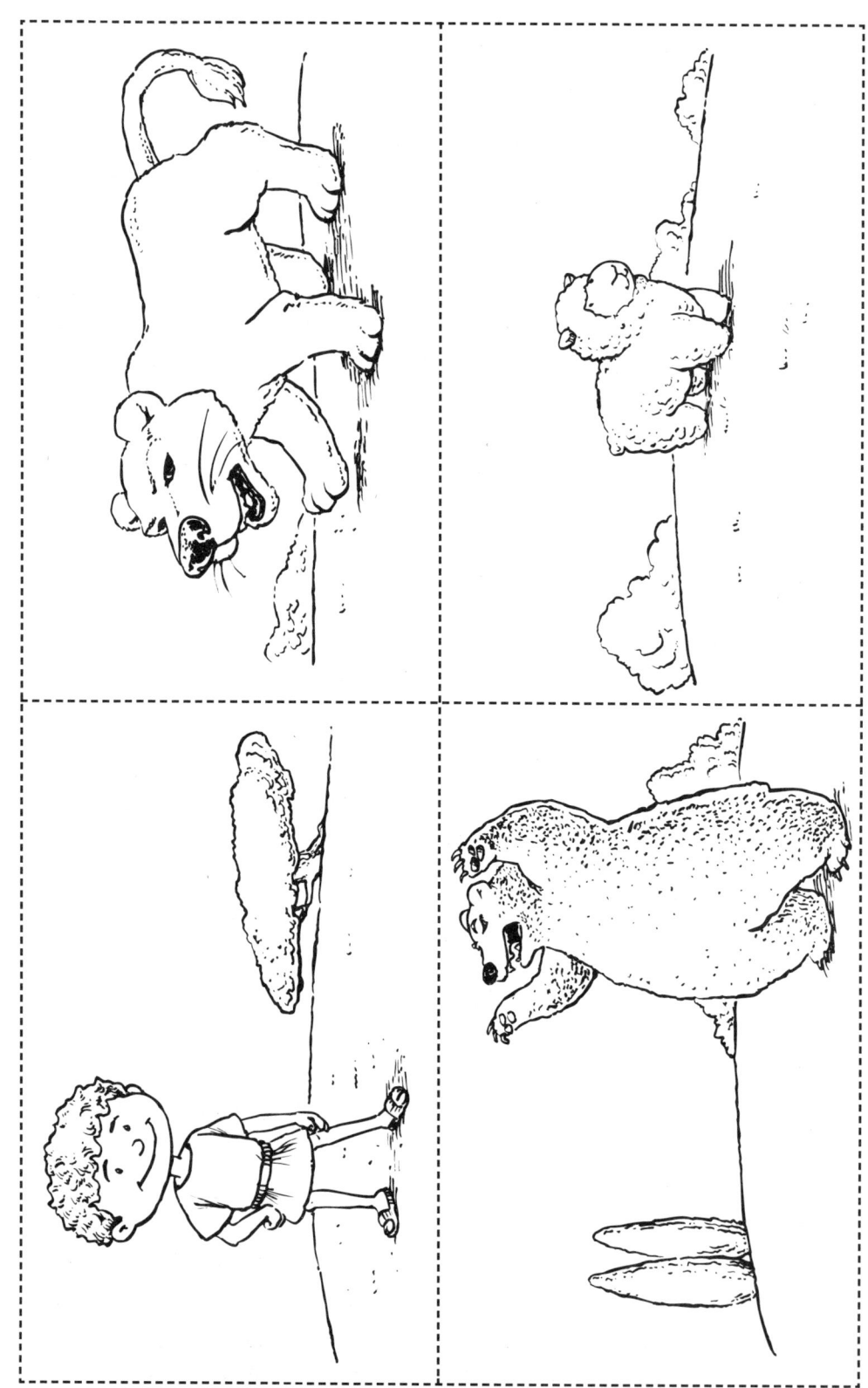

Where? Set four to six chairs around a table. Spread out the newsprint on the table. Place the damp sponge on the paper plate, and work some paint into it. Set the sponge where it is accessible to all the children. Give the paper, the remaining paint, and the paintbrush to an adult who will be your helper.

How? Show the children how to make little "footprints" using their hands. Have each child make a fist and press the pinky side of the fist into the paint in the sponge. Show them how to make the print on the newsprint that is covering the table. They can add "toes" with the tips of their pinky fingers dipped in paint.

As children are practicing making these little footprints, have the helper work with one child at a time to remove a shoe, paint the bare foot with the sponge paintbrush, and make a print on a piece of construction paper. Use damp paper towels to wipe the paint off the children's feet. Each child can then take the big footprint back to the table and make a little footprint beside it on the paper.

Magnifying Glass Exploration

Science and Nature

To Do and To Notice—*Use a magnifying glass to remember that God's power made David able to do a big job.*

As the children work, you can ask them these questions:
- **How does the magnifying glass change the way the objects look?**
- **Does anything look particularly interesting or beautiful when you look at it through the magnifying glass?**
- **The magnifying glass makes things seem bigger than they really are. Was there something that made David able to do a big job? What was it?**
- **What big things can God help you do?**

What? You'll need six place mats, one or more magnifying glasses, and six different types of items to view (such as small rocks with varying textures; leaves, flowers, and twigs; crackers and cereal; pieces of fruits and vegetables; coins and small pieces of written material from newspapers or magazines; and paper clips, brass fasteners, and rubber bands).

Where? Put the place mats on a table that the children can easily circulate around. Place one of the groups of items listed in the supplies on each of the place mats. Place the magnifying glasses around the table for the children to share.

How? As you introduce the center, show the children how to focus a magnifying glass. Encourage them to explore the items at each workspace and observe how the magnifying glass changes the appearance of the items. Encourage them to also explore their friends' faces and hair, their own shoes, or other items.

Abigail Prevents Trouble
1 Samuel 25

In this story, Abigail shows not only the good judgment that David praised her for but also tremendous resolve and bravery in going out to meet him on the road. In doing so, she saved David from the sins of revenge and murder and saved her people from destruction at his hands.

After telling the story, use these centers to help your children become familiar with the story of Abigail and her example of wisdom and generosity.

In Abigail's Tent
Dramatic and Imaginative Play

To Do and To Notice—*Pack supplies inside a tent to experience what it might have been like for Abigail to prepare to meet David.*

As the children work, you can ask them these questions:
- **How does it feel to make and pack food while inside a tent?**
- **Why do you think Abigail wanted to give David gifts?**
- **If you had been Abigail, how would you have carried all of the food to David and his men?**

What? You'll need a large bedsheet, a table, plastic foods, various sizes of scarves or fabric squares, rope, and a box.

Where? Choose an area of the room that has enough space for children to freely move around the table. Drape the sheet over the table to form a tent, and place the rest of the supplies under the table.

How? As you introduce the center, choose a child to help you show the others how to put items in the center of a piece of fabric, draw the sides closed, and tie it with a rope. One person can hold the fabric while the other ties the rope. Explain that this is similar to what Abigail might have done to prepare the supplies for David's men, since she didn't have bags in which to pack things. Encourage the children to prepare lots of supply packs for David's men and to think about how the men would carry all of the food. Preschoolers can make small packs of supplies for one person or larger packs for groups of people. Have children appoint one person to count the supplies and one person to pack them all in a box. Then have children pretend to take the supplies to David's men. Afterward, they can switch roles and pretend to be David's men receiving and unpacking the gifts to make them ready for the next group.

Protecting Nabal's Sheep
Arts and Crafts

To Do and To Notice—*Make sheep puppets and remember the way that David served Nabal and protected his wealth.*

As the children work, you can ask them these questions:
- **What do you think David and his men did to take care of the sheep?**
- **Why do you think David protected Nabal's sheep?**
- **What do you think Nabal should have done for David?**

What? You'll need photocopies of the sheep patterns below, glue sticks, cotton balls, craft sticks, and green modeling dough. (You may want to make modeling dough using the recipe on page 108.) Have enough supplies for each child to make four sheep puppets.

Where? Set up a table and four to six chairs. Place four sheep cutouts and a glue stick at each workspace. Put the cotton, craft sticks, and modeling dough where they are accessible to all the children.

Permission to photocopy this handout from *Wiggly, Giggly Bible Learning Centers for Preschoolers* granted for local church use. Copyright © Group Publishing, Inc, P.O. Box 481, Loveland, CO 80539.

How? Make a model of the sheep stick puppets before class. As you introduce this center, show the children how to spread glue on the sheep cutouts, then put several cotton balls on each one. Explain that the kids will then glue each sheep to a craft stick to make small puppets. Encourage kids to make four puppets each. Then they can stick their sheep in the green modeling dough and pretend the sheep are standing on a grassy hill. Encourage children to discuss how they might have cared for and protected the sheep if they had been David's men.

Lots of Loaves
Home and Life Skills

To Do and To Notice—*Knead bread dough and make loaves to appreciate how much bread Abigail packed.*

As the children work, you can ask them these questions:
- **How many tables do you think it would take to hold two hundred loaves of bread?**
- **What does the dough smell like?**
- **What are some of the differences between the dough and the bread?**
- **What are some kinds of food you would share with a guest?**

Around the Corner

Yeast dough has a different texture than other types of dough. Show several different varieties of yeast breads, pointing out their different shapes. It's fun to share with children breads made in different parts of the world and to let them sample several different kinds. If you observe all the proper sanitary conditions, you could bake the loaves of each group separately and allow the children to snack on the bread later.

What? Put about four pounds of defrosted bread dough in a large plastic bowl. (You may purchase frozen dough from the grocery store or make your own yeast dough.) You'll also need a loaf of French bread and a package of small soft rolls.

Where? Set up a table or bench with enough space around it for the children to circulate freely. Put the bowl of dough, the French bread, and the rolls on the table.

How? As you introduce the center, tell the children about the different shapes that the same bread dough can be made into. Show children the loaf of French bread and one of the soft rolls. Then show kids the bowl of dough, and (based on the information on the package) tell them how many loaves of bread it would make. Tell children how many bowls of dough it would take to make two hundred loaves.

Show the children how to knead the dough in the bowl and how to shape a small amount of the dough into a little loaf. Have the children take turns kneading the bread dough and exploring its unique qualities, including its smell and texture. After all the children have had a turn, let them make small loaves until all the dough is used up. Encourage them to count the little loaves. When they have finished, they can return the loaves to the bowl and knead the dough again, getting it ready for the next group.

Something to Share

Readiness

> **To Do and To Notice**—*Share puzzle pieces to construct circular, magnetic puzzles.*

As the children work, you can ask them these questions:
- **How does your sharing help others as you work together?**
- **What would happen if someone wouldn't share with the rest of the group?**
- **Why is sharing important?**
- **What do you think Nabal learned about sharing from Abigail?**

What? You'll need six 8-inch circles, each cut from a different color of paper; self-adhesive magnet strips; six envelopes; scissors; and three cookie sheets.

Where? Lean the cookie sheets against a wall. Spread out a large blanket in front of the wall to define the center area. Cut each circle into six equal pieces, and put a strip of magnet on the back of each piece. Then put one piece of each color circle into each of the six envelopes. Prop the envelopes against the cookie sheets.

How? As you introduce the center, explain to the children that inside each envelope are pieces from each of six different-colored circle puzzles. Give each child an envelope. To make one circle of each color, they will need to share the pieces found in each envelope. Using the contents of one envelope, start each of the six circles, showing the children how to place the pieces on the cookie sheets. Allow the children to develop their own strategies for completing the task of making six complete, single-colored circles. When kids have finished, ask them to return the pieces to the envelopes for the next group, being careful to put one of each color inside each envelope. If they have extra time, the children can experiment with making circles of different colors. Encourage patterning or developing circles that are half one color, half another.

Nathan the Prophet— A King's Best Friend
2 Samuel 7; 12

Nathan pops in and out of the Old Testament as a wise whisperer. He was King David's personal prophet, speaking words both tough and tender for God.

Tell the story, then use these centers to help the children learn that the prophet Nathan carried God's words to the king even though the messages were sometimes tough to hear. Preschoolers can learn about loyalty to God and to friends by following Nathan's wise example.

A Message to Be Heard
Listening and Music

To Do and To Notice—*Record messages on a tape recorder and play them back to remember Nathan's important message for King David.*

As the children work, you can ask them these questions:
- **What do you like about recording your messages?**
- **Who do you think remembered Nathan's message?**
- **What kind of messages do you like to share with others?**
- **How do you think Nathan felt about having to give the king the message that God was not happy with him?**

What? You'll need a tape recorder and a blank tape.

Where? Set the tape recorder on a carpeted area of the floor, away from other centers.

How? Show the children how to use the tape recorder to record their own words. Encourage children to tape themselves; they can pass along any information or message they wish. Tell them they may speak or sing into the microphone. Encourage the children not to give their names as they record the messages. After all the messages have been recorded, let the children rewind the tape to different points and try to identify who is speaking.

Nathan Names a Baby
Games

To Do and To Notice—*Play a game to celebrate Nathan's happy message from God.*

After the game, you can ask children these questions:
- **Who do you think named you?**
- **When have you had a happy message? What was the message?**

What? You'll need masking tape, a blanket, and a baby doll.

Where? Choose a large, open area of the room, and put a line of masking tape in the center of the area.

How? As you introduce this game, remind the children that the happiest message Nathan gave David was what to name his baby son. God told David, through Nathan, to give the baby a name that means "loved by the Lord."

Set the baby doll in the middle of the blanket, and show the children how to carry the baby by pulling the blanket across the floor. Appoint one child to be the prophet, and have him or her stand at one end of the center area. Have the other children stand at the opposite end, leaving the baby and blanket on the line in the middle of the playing area. The prophet will call out, "Name the baby [child's name]," naming a person standing on the other side of the room. The person whose name was called will run up to the blanket and pull the baby to the child playing the prophet. The prophet will pull the blanket and the doll back to the line and join the children at the other side of the center. The child whose name was called will become the new prophet. The baby must remain on the blanket at all times. Play this game with the children until they get the idea. Then they can play independently.

Carrying a Message
Blocks and Construction

To Do and To Notice—*Work together to build a block structure to learn about the importance of carrying messages.*

As the children work, you can ask them these questions:
- **Is the builder's job or the carrier's job more important? Why?**
- **David's job was important, but could he do it alone? Why or why not?**
- **Were all the blocks helpful, or did some slow your building down?**

- **How do you think Nathan felt about having to carry a sad message to David?**

What? You'll need a stopwatch and different-shaped building blocks.

Where? Designate an 8-foot-long area for this center. Put a table at one end, and put the blocks at the other end. Put the stopwatch on the table.

How? Remind the children that Nathan obeyed God by carrying God's message to King David. Choose one child to be the king, who is trying to build a kingdom at the table. Explain that the rest of the children will be messengers, carrying blocks to the king. Show the kids how to use the stopwatch. Let the child playing the king start the stopwatch to show the messengers that he or she is ready to build. Each child may pick up a block and carry it to the king. As soon as his or her block is in place, the child will return to the block pile for another block. When all the blocks are in place, the king can announce the numbers on the stopwatch. Choose another child to be the king and play this building game again. Encourage children to play the game more quickly each time.

Love Letters
Readiness

> **To Do and To Notice**—*Write and mail letters containing a message about God.*

As the children work, you can ask them these questions:
- **What are some things you think God wants people to know?**
- **What are some ways God gets his messages across today?**
- **Who can be a messenger for God?**

What? You'll need stationery, envelopes, labels printed with the message "God Loves You," postage stamps, the children's addresses (preprinted on labels, if possible), various writing tools (pens, pencils, crayons, or markers), and a box with a slit cut in it to serve as a mailbox.

Where? Set up a table and four to six chairs. Put a piece of stationery, an envelope, and a printed label at each workspace. Place the rest of the supplies where they are accessible to each child.

How? As you introduce this center, remind the children that God still uses people to deliver his important messages. Explain that they will be writing letters to their families with an important message about God. Allow the children to write their letters as well as they can and affix the "God Loves You" message to the papers. Show them how to fold the stationery to fit in the envelope, and let them prepare their envelopes for mailing. (You may wish to let the children pretend to affix stamps and place the real ones yourself.) When the children have finished, they can drop their letters in the box provided. You can then put real stamps on the envelopes and mail them.

King Solomon—A Wise and Wealthy King
1 Kings 3, 2 Chronicles 1–4; 9

King Solomon became the one of the wisest and wealthiest men who ever lived. God blessed him because he started his reign with a humble request. God granted King Solomon his request for wisdom, and God also blessed him with jewels, gold, and horses. After telling the story, use these centers to help children learn that wisdom is more important than any earthly treasure.

A Temple With Treasures
Cooking

To Do and To Notice—*Make a yummy treat to remember that God gave King Solomon wisdom to rule his kingdom and treasures for the Temple.*

As the children work, you can ask them these questions:
- Why do you think King Solomon asked God for wisdom?
- How did God answer King Solomon's prayers?
- What do you think King Solomon remembered when he looked at his treasures?

What? You'll need graham crackers, fruit-flavored cream cheese, fruit cocktail (drained and dried with a paper towel), plastic knives, paper plates, and napkins.

Where? Set up a table and four to six chairs. Place a paper plate, plastic knife, and napkin at each workspace. Set the other items on a table where all the kids can reach them.

How? Remind the children that King Solomon gave orders to his people to build the Temple in the name of the Lord. Make a model of this snack as you introduce the center. Show the children how to spread cream cheese on a cracker and stick another cracker to it. Show them how to use four square crackers to make a three-sided temple with a roof. Let them place pieces of fruit cocktail inside of the temple to represent Solomon's jewels. Place the completed model in the center to remind children how to make the snack.

King Solomon's Treasure
Readiness

To Do and To Notice—*Sort "precious treasure" as a reminder of the wealth that God blessed King Solomon with.*

As the children work, you can ask them these questions:
- **What were the things God gave King Solomon?**
- **What kinds of "treasure" do you have at home?**
- **How can we show God our thanks for the blessings he gives us?**

What? You'll need small rocks spray painted gold, red, green, and purple (an equal number of each color); and small baskets or boxes.

Where? Place all of the painted rocks on a small table that the children can easily walk around.

How? Remind children that God gave King Solomon enormous riches because the king did not ask for wealth but instead he asked God for wisdom to rule his kingdom. Have the children pretend to be King Solomon's workers in the palace who must count and sort the treasure. Encourage the children to work together to sort the treasures into like groups using the baskets or boxes provided.

King Solomon's Horses
Arts and Crafts

To Do and To Notice—*Make horses from paper bags to remember Solomon's wealth.*

As the children work, you can ask them these questions:
- **How many horses do you think King Solomon had?**
- **What kinds of needs did King Solomon's horses have?**
- **Who do you think took care of those needs?**
- **Who takes care of your needs?**

What? You'll need lunch bags, yarn cut into various lengths, newspaper, 2-inch triangles cut from grocery bags, large wiggly eyes (or 1½-inch white circles each with a ½-inch black dot in the center), crayons, and glue.

Where? Place the items on a low table within reach of the children.

How? Make a model of this project before class. Show the model to the kids, and then show them how to crumple newspaper to stuff inside a lunch bag and tape the bag shut. Bend the bag in the middle of the long, narrow side, pushing the original bottom of the bag forward to create the illusion of a head and a neck. Let the kids decorate the bottom of the bag, gluing on triangles for the ears, yarn pieces between the ears for the mane, and the eyes. Color in nostrils at the edge of the bag. Let each child name his or her horse and tell how it should be cared for.

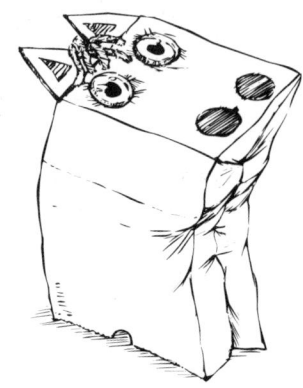

A King's Crown
Arts and Crafts

To Do and To Notice—*Make a crown to remember how King Solomon wisely ruled his kingdom.*

As the children work, you can ask them these questions:
- **Why would a king need wisdom?**
- **What do you think was the wisest thing King Solomon ever did?**
- **Why might you need wisdom in your life?**

What? You'll need crowns cut from heavy tagboard, 2-inch tissue paper squares, colored fruit-cereal pieces, two or three different colors of dry gelatin in saltshakers, glue, and a stapler.

Where? Place four to six chairs around a small table. Place a crown at each workspace. Put the rest of the supplies where they are easily accessible to the children.

How? Show the children how to decorate a crown with the materials provided. Have them glue on tissue paper squares and cereal pieces. Then draw lines with the glue and sprinkle dry gelatin on the glue lines. This activity will be easier for the kids to do while the crowns are still flat. When the crowns are completely dry, staple the ends of each crown together to fit the child's head.

Queen of Sheba— The Inquiring Queen Visits the Wise King

1 Kings 10:1-10, 13; 2 Chronicles 9:1-9, 12

The queen of Sheba heard about King Solomon's wisdom and his knowledge of the true God of Israel. As the queen of another country, she was brave to travel such a distance, generous to bring such a wealth of gifts, and humble to seek wisdom from another sovereign.

After telling the story, use these centers to help preschoolers explore and discover truths about the story of the queen of Sheba and how she learned to acknowledge the awesome God who blesses his people.

On the Road With Royalty
Home and Life Skills

To Do and To Notice—*Prepare to travel a long distance as the queen of Sheba did before she visited Solomon.*

As the children work, you can ask them these questions:
- **How do you know what to take on a long trip?**
- **What do you think the queen of Sheba packed for her trip?**
- **Tell about a trip you have taken with your family.**

What? You'll need small suitcases, backpacks, or small boxes; doll clothes or children's clothes; dishes; toys; and play food.

Where? If you have a home center, allow the children to use other supplies from that area. If not, place all the supplies in a corner of the room where children have enough space to move freely.

How? As you introduce this center, remind children that the queen traveled a long way to see King Solomon. Encourage kids to talk about things they might need if they were going on a long trip with no restaurants or gas stations to stop at along the way. Also encourage them to think about gifts that they might want to take with them. Allow the children to pack the suitcases and boxes, working together or alone.

Around the Corner

For added fun, turn this activity into a relay in which a child packs a suitcase, carries it to another area, and unpacks it. Then the next child in the relay repacks the suitcase and carries it back.

Gems and Jewels
Arts and Crafts

> **To Do and To Notice**—*Create necklaces using "jewels" the queen might have brought to King Solomon.*

As the children work, you can ask them these questions:
- **What kinds of gifts do you like to give to others?**
- **What gifts have you received that you really liked?**
- **How do you think the king felt when he received all the gifts the queen brought to him?**

What? You'll need an 18-inch length of yarn or gold cord for each child, buttons with large holes and tubular pasta for stringing, and tape. Prepare the yarn or cord by wrapping a small piece of tape around one end to make it easier to slide the string through the holes in the objects. Tie a knot at the other end of each string.

Where? Set up a table with four to six chairs. Place one of the prepared strings and a pile of the stringing items at each workspace.

How? Explain to children that the queen of Sheba brought beautiful jewels to the king. Show children how to begin stringing their necklaces. Encourage them to create patterns as they string the items. When they get to the ends of their strings, tie the necklaces into circles. Let the children wear or trade their necklaces when they have finished making them.

Pretend Palaces
Blocks and Construction

> **To Do and To Notice**—*Build "palaces" like the home the queen of Sheba might have lived in.*

As the children work, you can ask them these questions:
- **Where do queens and kings live?**
- **What do kings and queens do?**
- **Who gives kings and queens wisdom to rule well?**

What? You'll need blocks, artificial greenery, 3-inch or longer cinnamon sticks, gem stickers, and small play people.

Where? Place the supplies in a large, open space where the children can move around freely.

How? As you introduce this center, allow the children to imagine what it might have been like to be a wealthy queen. Point out the greenery, gem stickers, and cinnamon sticks as items that represent the queen's wealth. Tell children they can use these items to adorn the palace. Allow the children to build a palace with the blocks and the items provided. Encourage them to use the play people as the royal inhabitants of their castle.

Around the Corner
Set out costume jewelry, gold garlands, and shiny fabric for the children to use to make the castle fancy enough for royalty.

Fortune Hunting
Science and Nature

To Do and To Notice—*Search for and find hidden "jewels."*

As the children play, you can ask them these questions:
- **What colors of jewels are you finding?**
- **What would you do with real jewels?**
- **Why do you think the queen brought jewels to the king?**
- **Which is more important—having lots of pretty jewels or having wisdom from God about how to live for him?**

What? You'll need several plastic bowls, a "treasure box," rice, and sequins.

Where? Set up a low table with enough space around it for the children to circulate freely. Place the bowls on the table, and fill each bowl with several cups of rice. Open a package of sequins and mix in the sequins with the rice. Put the treasure box where all the children can reach it.

How? As you introduce this center, explain to the children that the queen of Sheba's jewels had to be mined from the ground by workers. Tell children they are going to pretend to be the queen's workers and search for jewels in the jewel pits. Show them how to sift the rice through their fingers, picking out the fancy sequins and placing them in the treasure box. Remind the children not to eat the uncooked rice.

Around the Corner
Show children some library books with pictures of gems in their natural state.

Elijah
1 Kings 18

Elijah was a prophet who was called upon to make the people decide if they were going to follow the one true God or fake gods. He set up a contest to show the people that they should follow God. When God sent down fire in answer to Elijah's prayer, the people decided to worship the one true God.

Tell children the story, and use these centers to help preschoolers explore the story of Elijah and how he helped people worship the one true God. Preschoolers can discover that they, too, have access to the awesome power of God.

Building an Altar
Wet and Dry

To Do and To Notice—*Pretend to build a trench around an altar to show how Elijah prepared to demonstrate the power of God.*

As the children work, you can ask them these questions:
- **Why do you think the offering Baal's servants made didn't burn?**
- **Why do you think Elijah dug a trench and poured water all over the altar?**
- **How do you think the fire burned even when everything was wet?**

What? You'll need twelve rocks (each about the size of a child's fist), a sandbox (or a dishpan of sand for every two children at the center), a plastic tablecloth, a spray bottle of water (use more water if it's practical in your setting), and a red mitten or fabric scrap. If you use several dishpans, you'll need twelve rocks for each pan.

Where? Place a plastic tablecloth on the floor beneath the sand play area, or use a sand table or sandbox outdoors.

How? Explain to the children that they are going to build a place like the altar Elijah set up for the sacrifice described in the Bible. Have the children count the twelve rocks as they stack them in the center of the sand. Then let children dig a trench around the altar. Have them spray water on the rocks, and remind them that Elijah used so much water that it filled the trench around the altar. Then, covering a hand with the red mitten or fabric, they can knock down the rock pile to show how God consumed Elijah's sacrifice by fire. Let the children rebuild and re-enact the story several times, taking turns wearing the red mitten.

Mix and Match
Readiness

> **To Do and To Notice**—*Play a matching game with pictures depicting the story of Elijah building an altar and calling out to God.*

Before the children search for the cards or when all the cards have been found you can ask:
- **What were rocks used for in the story?**
- **What was poured on the altar? Why?**
- **What burned up the sacrifice? Where did it come from?**
- **How do you think Elijah felt about God?**
- **What did the servants of Baal learn when Elijah's sacrifice to God burned?**

What? You'll need two sets of the pictures on page 90 and masking tape. Glue each of the pictures to a 3x5-inch index card.

Where? Choose an area of the room in which to hide the pictures. Designate the boundaries of this area with masking tape on the floor.

How? Before class, hide one set of the pictures. Give each child one of the pictures from the second set as he or she arrives at the center. Encourage kids to find the picture that matches the one they have. As children find a matching picture, they may remove the picture from its hiding space and sit down on the floor. Tell children that if they discover a picture that doesn't match the one they are holding, they should return the picture to its hiding spot.

God Hears Us When We Call Him
Prayer and Worship

> **To Do and To Notice**—*Gather for a special time of understanding that God hears our prayers.*

As the children work, you can ask them these questions:
- **Who is God? What does he do?**
- **What did God do when Elijah called out to God?**
- **Why do people in your church or family pray to God?**
- **What do you want God to hear from you today?**

Mix and Match

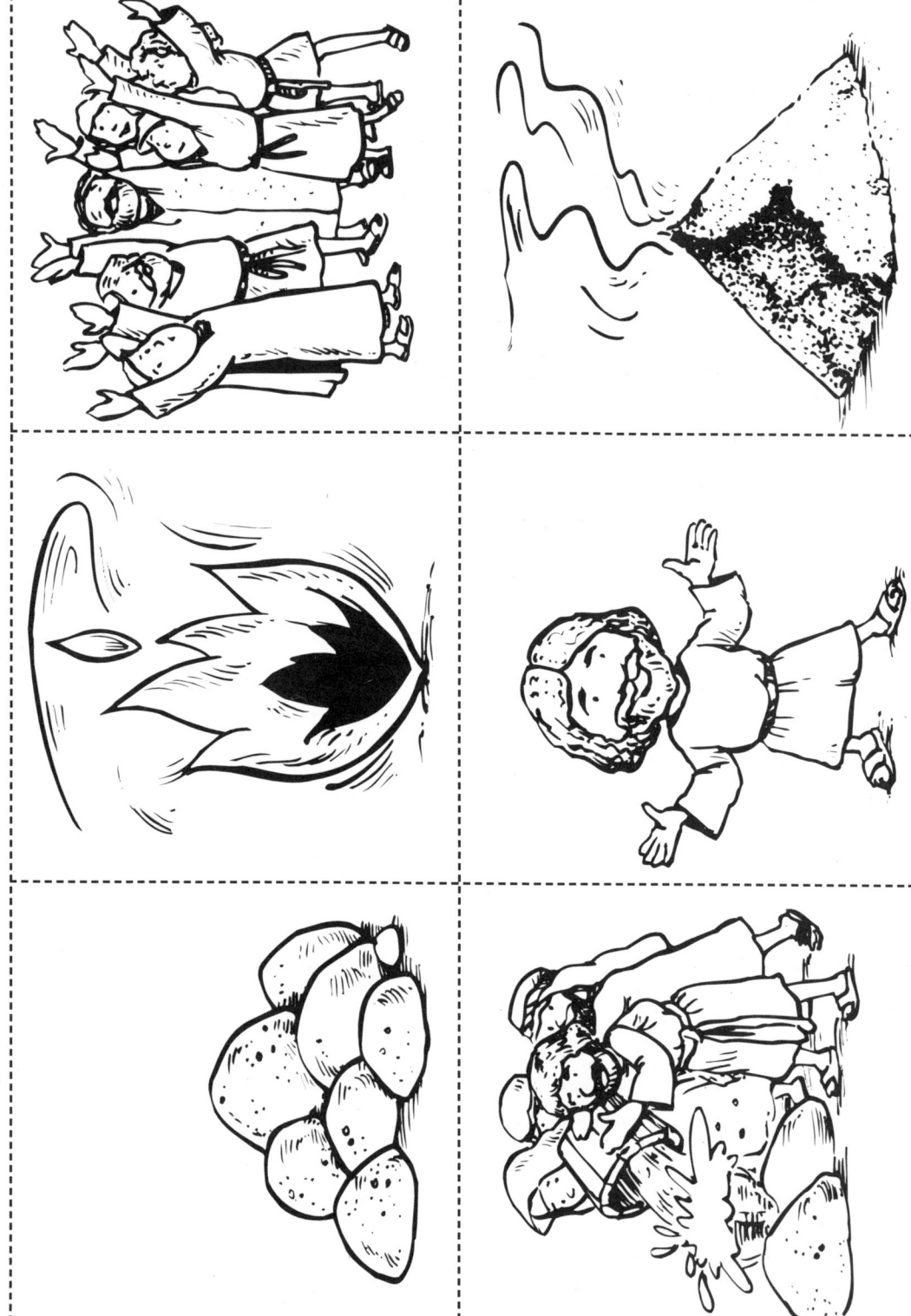

What? You'll need four to six rocks and a box with a lid.

Where? Place the rocks in the box. Set the box in a quiet corner of the room or in a nearby room.

How? Have a helper take the children to this center and explain that Elijah's story shows that our God hears and does things for people who call on him. Remind the children that God answered Elijah's prayer at an altar made of stones. Let children each take a rock from the box and hold it as they pray a simple prayer of request or thanksgiving. Then have the children return the rocks to the box to remind them that God is always ready to listen to us.

> **Around the Corner**
>
> This center requires a bit more adult direction than most. You may wish to seek out some extra helpers to direct children in this center.

Flame for God
Arts and Crafts

> **To Do and To Notice**—*Create a "fire" picture to remind children to worship God.*

As the children work, you can ask them these questions:
- **Why did God send the fire on Elijah's altar?**
- **Do you have special places to worship God at your house?**
- **How can you remember to worship God and tell him you love him?**

What? You'll need plastic wrap; tape; glue (diluted with an equal part of water); foam paintbrushes; red, yellow, and orange tissue paper cut into 2-inch squares; and yarn.

Where? Set up a table and four to six chairs. Tape a piece of plastic wrap at each workspace, and place a foam paintbrush beside it. Place the diluted glue and tissues so that all children can easily reach them.

How? As you introduce this center, remind the children that all the people worshipped God when they saw the fire God sent from heaven. Explain to the children that they will make fire pictures to hang in the classroom to remind them to worship God. Show children how to brush the glue all over their plastic wrap and lay the colored squares of tissue paper over the top. The squares should overlap. Then have the children paint another layer of glue over the top of the tissues. Encourage the children to tell God how much they love him as they work, and to think about places they might put their pictures so that they will remember to worship God often. When the glue is dry, peel the tissues away from the plastic wrap and discard the plastic wrap. The tissues may be cut into a flame shape, if desired. Use yarn to hang up the pictures in the room.

Naaman's Servant Girl
2 Kings 5:1-13

Naaman was a prominent army commander, a valiant soldier who was highly regarded and had been victorious in battle. In spite of his success, Naaman was doomed because he had leprosy. If it weren't for the faith of his wife's young slave, it's likely that Naaman would have died alone and in agony. However, this child—who had been taken from her homeland and made a slave—selflessly shared her faith in God. As a result, the prophet Elisha healed Naaman in the name of God.

After telling the story, use these centers to help children understand Naaman's plight and the miracle that happened when Naaman's servant girl shared her faith in a loving God.

Muddy River Cure
Arts and Crafts

To Do and To Notice—*Finger-paint with chocolate pudding to make a Jordan River scene.*

As the children work, you can ask them these questions:
- **Why do you think Naaman would not want to go into the river?**
- **How do you think Naaman felt about being so sick?**
- **What did God do for Naaman?**
- **How is the chocolate pudding like the water of the Jordan River? How is it different?**

What? You'll need protective coverings, chocolate pudding, finger painting paper, and copies of the Naaman figure on page 96 (precut).

Where? Set up a large table and four to six chairs near a sink, if possible. Place a sheet of finger painting paper and a Naaman figure at each workspace. Put about a teaspoon of chocolate pudding in the center of each paper.

How? Dress children in protective coverings, and have kids wash their hands. Then allow children to smear the pudding all over their papers. Encourage them to make the pudding look like river water. Allow the children to lick their fingers if they want to. When they have finished painting, they can each put a Naaman figure on the painted page. Make sure the children wash their hands when they have finished.

First First-Aid Kits
Home and Life Skills

To Do and To Notice—*Make a simple first-aid kit to share God's good news with others.*

As the children work, you can ask them these questions:
- **Have you ever told someone about God? What happened?**
- **Have you ever visited or prayed for someone who was sick?**
- **What things, besides bandages, help people who are hurt or sick?**

What? You'll need small (#6) envelopes, photocopies of the message on page 94, scissors, glue sticks, crayons, adhesive bandages, and individual antiseptic wipes (optional).

Where? Set up a table and four to six chairs. Put an envelope, scissors, and a photocopied message at each workspace. Place the other supplies where they are accessible to each child.

How? As you introduce this center, talk to the children about how to care for an injury. Explain that Naaman's illness was very bad, and that Naaman's servant girl told him how he could be cured. Explain that the children will be making simple first-aid kits with a message about God to share with people they know. Read the message to them. Encourage the children to be like Naaman's servant girl and tell others about God's love. Each child can cut out the message and glue it to an envelope. Younger children may require assistance with cutting. Then kids can color or draw on the back side of their envelopes. After they have finished, they can place one adhesive bandage and one antiseptic wipe in each envelope and seal it.

A Message With a Point
Small Motor Skills

To Do and To Notice—*Use modeling dough and practice saying the message from Naaman's servant girl.*

As the children work, you can ask them these questions:
- **Have you ever been sick? Who cared for you? What did you have to do before you were well?**
- **What is the worst part of being sick?**
- **What do you want to do when someone near you is sick?**
- **What do you think Naaman's servant girl wanted to do for Naaman?**

First-Aid Kits

I'm giving you this bandage
'Cause I want you to know
That my God is a healing God,
And I love God so!

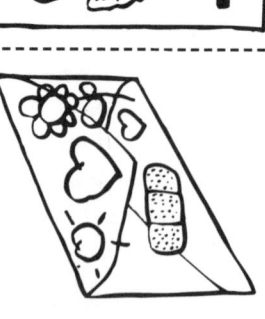

What? You'll need modeling dough (make your own from the recipe on page 108), cotton swabs, and a small bowl of water.

Where? Set up a table with four to six chairs around it. Place all the supplies where they are accessible to each child.

How? As you introduce this center, remind the children of the message the servant girl had for her master, Naaman. Show the children how they can sculpt Naaman from modeling dough. Encourage them to use the swabs to poke holes in the figure to resemble Naaman's leprosy spots. Then show them how to dip a cotton swab in water and rub it over the holes to fill them up and make the area smooth again. Each time they fill in a hole, encourage the children to say, "If only you would go, God would cure you like so!"

God Heals Pocket Book
Storytelling

> **To Do and To Notice**—*Using a book made from coffee filters, tell the story of Naaman.*

As the children work, you can ask them these questions:
- **Why do you think Naaman believed God?**
- **How do you think Naaman felt as he dunked himself in the river seven times?**
- **How do you think Naaman felt when he looked at his skin after the last dunk?**

What? You'll need cone-shaped coffee filters, stacked in groups of seven and stapled at the bottom sealed edge (one stack of filters per child); photocopies of the picture of Naaman on page 96 (two per child); scissors; and crayons.

Where? Set up a table and four to six chairs. Place a coffee-filter "book," two copies of the Naaman figure, and a pair of scissors at each workspace. Place the crayons where they are accessible to all the children.

How? As you introduce the center, show the children a pocket book you have assembled before class. Direct the children to color their pictures of Naaman, making them identical except for leprosy spots on one of them, and to cut them out. The children can color each of the filters brown to represent the muddy Jordan River. Have them hide the healed Naaman in

the seventh cone. Show the kids how to place the sick Naaman inside each of the pockets and to withdraw the healed Naaman from the seventh cone. Remind the children that the healed Naaman prayed and thanked God for making him well again. Let them practice retelling the story to other children in the center.

Naaman

Permission to photocopy this picture from *Wiggly, Giggly Bible Learning Centers for Preschoolers* granted for local church use. Copyright © Group Publishing, Inc., P.O. Box 481, Loveland, CO, 80539.

Esther—God's Chosen Queen
Esther 2–8

The story of Esther is a clear example of how God can use the most unlikely individuals to do amazing things. When Esther—an orphan and a Jew—was chosen over many beautiful women to be King Xerxes' queen, she was placed in a privileged and precarious position. God used Esther's bravery, faithfulness, and bold actions to save thousands of lives.

After telling the story, use these centers to provide many ways for preschoolers to discover how God used Esther to keep his people safe. Your children can discover that God has made them special and has created them for unique purposes, too.

Crown the Queen
Games

To Do and To Notice—*Play a game to remember that Esther was specially chosen to be the queen.*

As the children work, you can ask them these questions:
- **Why do you think God let Esther be queen?**
- **How did God make Esther special?**
- **What is something special about you?**
- **What is something special you can do for God?**

What? You'll need a crown or other head covering.

Where? Set aside a large, open area of the room for this center. You can mark boundary lines with masking tape if you wish.

How? As you introduce the center, remind the children that Esther was specially chosen to be the queen so that she could help save her people. Have the children sit on the floor in a large circle, and teach them this chant:

Esther, Esther, bold and brave,
Queen of the people you helped to save.

Show the children the crown or head covering you've chosen. Walk around behind the circle of children and place the head covering on someone's head as the children continue to chant. Encourage the selected child to chase you around the circle (walking fast, without running) and to try to catch you before you are able to sit in his or her vacated spot. Play a couple of times, then show children the area where they can play the game.

King's Scepters
Cooking

> **To Do and To Notice**—*Make a snack to share with family and friends to remember how brave Esther was when she went before the king.*

As the children work, you can ask them these questions
- **What did it mean for the king to hold out his scepter?**
- **Who are you afraid to talk to?**
- **What helps you to be brave?**

What? You'll need pretzel sticks, yellow cheese slices, plastic knives, paper plates, and resealable snack bags.

Where? Set up a table and four to six chairs near a hand-washing station. Put a paper plate and two slices of cheese at each workspace.

How? Make a model before class. Cut cheese slices into 1-inch squares. Lay four cheese squares, one on top of the other, at forty-five degree angles to make a multi-pointed, star-shaped block of cheese. Poke a pretzel stick into the center of each star. As you introduce the center, show the kids the pretty star on the end of the scepter, and remind the children that Esther had to see the king's gold scepter to know that she could go in and talk to him. Show kids how to cut up the cheese on a paper plate and place it to make the star, and then have them insert a pretzel. Allow the children to make scepters of different shapes and sizes, and then have kids put the snacks in plastic bags to take home and share with their families.

A Big Banquet
Home and Life Skills

> **To Do and To Notice**—*Paste pictures of banquet food on paper plates to remember the special meals Esther prepared in the palace.*

As the children work, you can ask them these questions:
- **Why do you think Esther invited people to dinner?**
- **When do you have special meals at your house?**
- **What kinds of things do you like to help cook?**

What? You'll need paper plates, glue sticks, and magazines with pictures of food.

Where? Set up a table and four to six chairs. Place the magazines on the table, and put a paper plate and glue stick at each workspace.

How? As you introduce the center, remind the children that Queen Esther wanted to prepare a wonderful meal for the king so that he'd be ready to hear her request. Explain that they can pretend to make a special meal for the king, loading his plate with yummy things to eat. Have the children take the magazines and tear out pictures of food they think a king might want to eat. After they have selected the pictures, they may glue them to a paper plate for the king. If they have time, they can create several plates of food for other guests. Let the children set the table and take turns pretending to be Queen Esther, serving the plates of food to other children in the center.

Esther Asks the King
Blocks and Construction

To Do and To Notice—*Create a castle or palace court to resemble the setting Queen Esther stood in to ask a favor of the king.*

As the children work, you can ask them these questions:
- **Why do you think Queen Esther was afraid to talk to the king?**
- **What helped Queen Esther be brave?**
- **What are some things that make you afraid?**
- **How can God help you be brave?**

What? You'll need masking tape, blocks, toy people, foil, and costume jewelry.

Where? Set up the supplies in an area of the floor marked off by masking tape.

How? Have children use blocks to create castles or palaces. Allow them to decorate their castles with foil and jewelry to make them beautiful like the palace Queen Esther lived in. Encourage the kids to use the toy figures to act out the Bible story, freeing Esther's people from Haman's mean plan.

Daniel Shows God's Power
Daniel 1; 3–6

Daniel, an exiled Jew who became a student in the Babylonian court, was committed to listening to God and being obedient. While in training for the king's service, Daniel obeyed God by refusing to eat foods deemed unclean for Jews. While in the king's service, Daniel interpreted the king's dreams and a message that was written on a wall. Daniel also survived being tossed into the lions' den—his punishment for continuing to pray to God in spite of the king's decree.

Enjoy using these centers to help your children discover that God can give them the same wisdom and power he gave Daniel to be brave and strong for God.

Wise Writers
Readiness

To Do and To Notice—*Write in salt to practice learning letters, as Daniel had to learn new letters when he came to Babylon.*

As the children work, you can ask them these questions:
- **How did it feel to draw letters in the salt?**
- **What do you think Daniel and his friends used to draw with when they were learning the letters of the Babylonian people?**
- **Do you think Daniel and his friends had to practice a long time before they could write in their new language? Why or why not?**
- **How could writing help you to serve God?**

Around the Corner
To reinforce the story of Daniel interpreting the writing on the wall, let the children copy letters from the cards on an outside wall, using a paintbrush and water. Or children can write on windows using wipe-off markers.

What? You'll need alphabet flash cards. (You may create your own by writing a different letter of the alphabet on each of twenty-six index cards, and gluing to each card a picture of an object that begins with the appropriate letter.) You'll also need four to six aluminum pie tins, each filled with one-half cup of salt, and a tarp.

Where? Set up a table or cover an area of the floor with a tarp. Place one letter card and one salt-filled pie tin at each workspace. Place the remainder of the cards where they are accessible to everyone.

How? Remind the children that God helped Daniel learn how to read and write when he was a young boy. Later, when Daniel lived in Babylon, he had to learn to read and write in the Babylonian language. Encourage your preschoolers to pray and ask God to help them learn how to read and write, too. Point out the pie tins and letter cards. Show children how to look at the flash cards and practice writing the letters in the salt; then have the children lightly shake the pie tins to create fresh canvases to practice on. Encourage the children to practice several different letters.

Exploring Good Foods
Science and Nature

To Do and To Notice—*Explore different vegetables to learn more about what Daniel and his friends ate.*

As the children work, you can ask them these questions:
- **Which vegetables do you enjoy eating?**
- **What happened to Daniel and his friends when they ate vegetables?**
- **What kinds of food help our bodies grow strong?**

What? You'll need paper plates; plastic spoons; a variety of thawed mixed vegetables, (try to include both familiar and unfamiliar blends, such as California-style vegetables or stew vegetables, and perhaps some small samples of individual vegetables); a serving spoon; and two large bowls. You may also wish to provide ranch dressing or other appropriate condiments.

Where? Set up a table close to a sink so children can easily wash their hands before and after they touch the vegetables. Put a selection of the vegetables in two bowls, one to sort from and one to taste from.

How? Explain to the children that Daniel and his friends believed God would make them strong and healthy even if they didn't eat food from the king's table. They chose to eat only vegetables. Point out the different vegetables, and allow the children to sort the vegetables from one of the bowls onto one or more paper plates. Each child can sort the vegetables by whatever criteria he or she wishes, such as kind of vegetable, color, hard and soft, or like and dislike. Encourage kids to feel, smell, and name each different vegetable in the bowl. After the children have explored and sorted the vegetables, return them to the bowl, and set the bowl aside. Offer samples from the serving bowl to eat with the condiments you have supplied.

Toasty Lions
Cooking

> **To Do and To Notice**—*Create a lion face by painting with milk on white bread and then toasting it.*

As the children work, you can ask them these questions:
- **Why do you think Daniel liked to pray?**
- **Why didn't the king want Daniel to be thrown in with the lions?**
- **What happened to Daniel when he was with the hungry lions?**
- **How can God help you be brave?**

What? You'll need a toaster oven; white bread; milk; three small bowls; yellow, red, and blue or green food coloring; paper plates; small, clean paintbrushes; butter or margarine; and plastic knives.

Where? Place a table against a wall that has an electrical outlet. Put the toaster oven on the table, and plug it in. (Make sure the toaster oven is out of the reach of the children.) Place four to six chairs at the table, and put a plastic place mat at each workspace. Mix one-quarter cup of milk with twenty-five drops of food coloring in each bowl. Put the bowls within reach of each child at the center.

How? Give each child a paper plate, a paintbrush, and a piece of white bread. Have bowls of different food coloring for every two to three children to share. Show the children how to paint a face in the center of the bread using the blue or green food coloring. Have them use the red and yellow colors to make lines all around the edge of their bread to create a lion's mane. Encourage the children to mix the yellow and red colors on their bread and watch what happens to the colors.

Set the toaster on the lightest setting. As each child finishes his or her lion creation, place the bread in the toaster oven and toast it lightly enough to allow the colors to show. When the toast is done, allow the children to spread butter or margarine on their lions and eat them.

Around the Corner

Make a grilled lion sandwich! Top a piece of plain bread with a slice of cheese. Put the lion bread on top, and toast the sandwich. Rrrroarin' good!

People of Praise
Prayer and Worship

To Do and To Notice—*Build block people and remember that God wants us to worship only him.*

As the children work, you can ask them these questions:
- **Why didn't Daniel and his friends worship the king's statue?**
- **Who does God want us to worship?**

What? You'll need masking tape and about ten blocks for each child.

Where? Use masking tape to create four to six 18-inch squares on the floor in a corner of the room (or use small carpet squares to define a workspace for each child). Place about ten blocks at each workspace.

How? Remind children that the king in the story of Daniel ordered all the people to worship a statue made from gold but God wants us to worship only him. Explain to children that they will build statues honoring God, because each part of the statues will represent one thing they can praise God for. Encourage the children to thank God for their feet as they place the blocks for the "feet" in their statues, and so on until they have praised God for every part of their bodies. Encourage the children to pray, "Help me to stand tall and worship only you, God." The children can remove the blocks and build other structures, praising God for something different each time they place a block.

Jonah Obeys God
Jonah 1–4

Jonah didn't just disobey; he did exactly the opposite of what God wanted him to do. He turned his back on God's directions. Preschoolers are old enough to begin to understand that the consequences of disobedience can be very unpleasant. But the real lesson here is about Jonah's willingness to repent and then obey.

God used Jonah's scary circumstances to bring Jonah back. After telling the story, use these centers to help your preschoolers understand that it's never too late to turn around and obey.

Inside the Big Fish
Dramatic and Imaginative Play

To Do and To Notice—*Review the story of Jonah and the big fish and pretend to be inside the fish's smelly belly.*

As the children work, you can ask them these questions:
- **How did it feel to be in the belly of the fish?**
- **How did it feel to pray as Jonah prayed in the fish's belly?**
- **What "stinky" circumstances have you found yourself in when you disobeyed? What happened?**

What? You'll need a refrigerator box (decorated to look like a fish if you wish), robes or towels for children to dress up in, a blue blanket or sheet, a can of sardines or fish oil, and construction paper for children to make other props such as seaweed or small fish.

Where? Place the box in an area of the room large enough to allow the children to play around and crawl through the box. Dab fish oil or oil from the sardines around the outer corners of the box. Place the construction paper and blanket near the box.

How? Remind the children of the story of Jonah. Encourage all the children to plan ahead to make construction paper props before they begin acting out the story. Stimulate their creativity by asking what Jonah might have had to share space with inside the fish. They can tear the paper to create fish, seaweed, or anything else that might make the story more realistic. Encourage them to take turns playing Jonah as he was swallowed by the big fish. Remind them that there were sailors and other passengers on the boat. Several children can play the parts of the sailors who tossed Jonah overboard. Once the child playing Jonah is inside the belly of the fish, he or she can pray as Jonah might have prayed and act out being spit up on the beach.

Belly-Goo Painting
Sensory Exploration

To Do and To Notice—*Finger-paint on corrugated cardboard to discover what it might have felt like to be inside the belly of a giant fish.*

As the children work, you can ask them these questions:
- **What do you think you would have done inside the belly of the fish?**
- **Why do you think the fish swallowed Jonah?**
- **What did Jonah learn from his time in the big fish?**

What? You'll need finger paint made from cornstarch, water, and lemon gelatin (see the recipe on page 108); corrugated cardboard or bulletin board covering; and wet wipes. You may also wish to provide protective coverings for the children.

Where? Set up a table surrounded by enough space for four to six children to stand comfortably. Cover the table with the corrugated cardboard or bulletin board covering. Keep the wet wipes nearby to wipe hands.

How? As you introduce the center, encourage the children to tell you what they think it might have felt like to be in the belly of a big fish. Tell them that they are going to be able to do some special finger painting to imagine what it might have been like to run their hands over the big fish's rib bones from the inside. Put a glob of the finger paint for each child somewhere on the corrugated cardboard, and encourage the children to rub their hands over it. You can also suggest that they count the "ribs," tickle the fish with their fingertips, or write their names as they imagine Jonah's experience inside the big fish.

Around the Corner

For extra fun, add seaweed products (found in health food stores) to the center for children to discover. You can make a smelly belly-goo by replacing the dissolved gelatin in the finger paint recipe (p. 108) with a can of water-packed tuna.

Jonah's Boat

Cooking

> **To Do and To Notice**—*Make edible boats and think about being on a little boat in the middle of a rough sea.*

As the children work, you can ask them these questions:
- **Why do you think God allowed the sea to get so rough?**
- **How would you feel if you were on a rough sea in a small boat?**
- **What caused the sea to become calm?**

What? You'll need paper plates, plastic knives, orange halves, crunchy mini-breadsticks, fruit leather, and soft-spread cream cheese.

Where? Set up a table and four to six chairs. Put a paper plate and a plastic knife at each workspace. Place the food supplies where they are accessible to all the children.

How? Make a model, showing the children how to poke a breadstick into the center of an orange half (you may have to push your finger down into the center of the orange first to widen the space). Show them how to use a plastic knife to cut a triangle sail from the fruit leather. Then spread cream cheese on the breadstick, and attach the fruit-leather triangle. Place the "boat" on a paper plate. Leave the model at the center to help children remember the directions. Encourage them to shake their paper plate "seas" and watch what happens to their little boats. When they have finished, they may eat the treats.

Story Pairs

Dramatic and Imaginative Play

> **To Do and To Notice**—*Using props, tell the story of Jonah to a partner.*

As the children work, you can ask them these questions:
- **How do you think Jonah felt when he was thrown overboard?**
- **What do you think Jonah did while he was in the belly of the fish?**
- **How do you think Jonah felt when he was spit onto dry land?**

What? You'll need three pieces of blue construction paper, three toy boats, nine small people figures (in groups of three), three little plastic bags of goldfish crackers, and three small boxes.

Where? Put one of each of the supplies in each of the three boxes, and set the boxes in an area where children can sit on the floor to work.

How? As you introduce the center, ask a child to help you demonstrate the story. Sit across from your partner. Put the blue construction paper on the floor between you. This will be the sea. Take the boat from the box, place it on the blue sea, and say that Jonah got into a boat because he didn't want to go where God told him to go. Take the people figures out of the box, and say that the sailors threw Jonah in with the fish. Put one of the people figures in the water, and scatter the fish crackers on the paper. Say that a big fish swallowed Jonah as you use the plastic bag to gobble up the play figure. Finally, tell the children that Jonah was ready to obey God, so the big fish spit Jonah out on the shore. Squeeze the bag, popping the figure onto the floor away from the blue construction paper. Return all the items to the box.

Tell the children to each pick a partner and take turns telling the story to each other using the items from the box in the same way you did.

Recipes

Modeling Dough

1½ cups flour
1½ cups salt
1 teaspoon powdered alum
1 cup boiling water
1 teaspoon vegetable oil
red or green food coloring

Mix the dry ingredients together. Add oil and water, and stir vigorously with a wooden spoon. Add food coloring as desired, and knead. This makes 2 cups of dough. Do not double this recipe for large amounts, but mix several recipes instead. This will keep for several months when stored in a tightly covered container. Objects made with these ingredients dry to a hard finish overnight. Add peppermint extract to scent the dough, if desired.

Finger Paint

1 cup cornstarch
1½ cups cool water
½ cup boiling water
1 package lemon gelatin
3 cups boiling water

Dissolve the gelatin in ½ cup of boiling water. Mix the cornstarch with the cool water in a medium-sized saucepan. Slowly add 3 cups boiling water to the cornstarch mixture, stirring constantly. Cook over medium heat, stirring constantly, until the mixture comes to a boil and is clear. Remove from heat, and stir in the gelatin mixture. Cool before using.

Butter Cookies

1½ cups powdered sugar
1 cup softened butter
1 egg
1 teaspoon vanilla
¾ teaspoon butter flavoring
2½ cups flour
1 teaspoon baking soda
1 teaspoon cream of tartar

Combine the first five ingredients. Mix in the remaining ingredients. Divide the dough in half. Roll each half into a log. Freeze the logs overnight. Cut 3/16-inch cookies from the logs, and bake 7 to 8 minutes at 375 degrees.

Index by Center Type

Arts and Crafts
Abigail 75
David 71
Deborah 49
Elijah 91
Hannah 63
Joseph 26
Joshua 38
Miriam 31
Naaman's Servant Girl 92
Queen of Sheba 86
Rahab 44
Rebekah 20
Sarah 15, 16
Solomon 83, 84

Blocks and Construction
Deborah 49
Esther 99
Moses 35
Nathan 79
Queen of Sheba 86
Rahab 42
Samuel 69

Cooking
Daniel 102
Esther 98
Jacob 25
Jonah 106
Noah 10
Rebekah 20
Solomon 82

Dramatic and Imaginative Play
Abigail 74
Gideon 53
Jacob 24
Jonah 104, 106
Joseph 27
Miriam 30
Moses 34
Rahab 44

Samson 55

Games
Esther 97
Joseph 27
Joshua 40
Nathan 79
Noah 11
Ruth 60
Samson 57

Home and Life Skills
Abigail 76
Esther 98
Gideon 53
Hannah 64, 65
Jacob 23
Miriam 32
Naaman's Servant Girl 93
Queen of Sheba 85
Ruth 60
Samson 56
Samuel 68

Listening and Music
David 70
Deborah 47
Gideon 54
Nathan 78
Samuel 68
Sarah 14

Prayer and Worship
Daniel 103
Deborah 48
Elijah 89
Hannah 65

Readiness
Abigail 77
Daniel 100
Elijah 89
Jacob 24

Joshua 39
Nathan 80
Rebekah 21
Solomon 83

Science and Nature
Daniel 101
David 73
Noah 12
Queen of Sheba 87
Ruth 61
Samson 56
Samuel 67

Sensory Exploration
Jonah 105
Sarah 15

Small Motor Skills
Moses 36
Naaman's Servant Girl 93
Rahab 45
Ruth 59

Storytelling
David 71
Joseph 28
Joshua 39
Moses 35
Naaman's Servant Girl 95
Rebekah 18

Wet and Dry
Elijah 88
Gideon 52
Miriam 32
Noah 11

Group Publishing, Inc.
Attention: Product Development
P.O. Box 481
Loveland, CO 80539
Fax: (970) 679-4370

Evaluation for
Wiggly, Giggly Bible Learning Centers for Preschoolers

Please help Group Publishing, Inc., continue to provide innovative and useful resources for ministry. Please take a moment to fill out this evaluation and mail or fax it to us. Thanks!

• • •

1. As a whole, this book has been (circle one)

not very helpful   very helpful

1   2   3   4   5   6   7   8   9   10

2. The best things about this book:

3. Ways this book could be improved:

4. Things I will change because of this book:

5. Other books I'd like to see Group publish in the future:

6. Would you be interested in field-testing future Group products and giving us your feedback? If so, please fill in the information below:

Name _____

Church Name _____

Denomination _____ Church Size_____

Church Address _____

City _____ State _____ ZIP _____

Church Phone _____

E-mail _____

Permission to photocopy this page granted for local church use.
Copyright © Group Publishing, Inc., P.O. Box 481, Loveland, CO 80539.

Exciting Resources for Your Children's Ministry

Wiggly, Giggly Bible Stories About Jesus

Delight your preschoolers with 25 foundational Bible stories from Jesus' life! You actually get 100 stories...because each of the 25 key stories features 4 distinct techniques for telling it! They will love hearing these 5- to 10-minute stories as you wrap Bible truths in finger plays, fun rhymes, motion songs, creative sound effects, puppet plays, and more!

ISBN 0-7644-2046-1

Wiggly, Giggly Bible Stories From the Old Testament

This delightful sequel to *Wiggly, Giggly Bible Stories About Jesus* brings 25 Old Testament heroes to life using simple, fun, and age-appropriate methods. Each 5- to 10-minute story features different activities to help preschoolers better understand the characters and the lessons they teach. They're easy and flexible to use in existing programs and are perfect for Sunday schools, preschools, and even for parents.

ISBN 0-7644-2145-X

Sunday School Specials Series

Lois Keffer

This best-selling series is a lifesaver for small churches that combine age groups...large churches that host family nights...and small groups with kids to entertain. Each book provides an entire quarter of active-learning experiences, interactive Bible stories, life applications, and take-home handouts. Children love them because they're fun and you'll love the easy preparation!

Sunday School Specials	ISBN 1-55945-082-7
Sunday School Specials 2	ISBN 1-55945-177-7
Sunday School Specials 3	ISBN 1-55945-606-X
Sunday School Specials 4	ISBN 0-7644-2050-X

The Children's Worker's Encyclopedia of Bible-Teaching Ideas

You get over 350 attention-grabbing, active-learning devotions...art and craft projects...creative prayers...service projects...field trips...music suggestions...quiet reflection activities...skits...and more—winning ideas from each and every book of the Bible! Simple, step-by-step directions and handy indexes make it easy to slide an idea into any meeting—on short notice—with little or no preparation!

Old Testament	ISBN 1-55945-622-1
New Testament	ISBN 1-55945-625-6

Order today from your local Christian bookstore, or write: Group Publishing, P.O. Box 485, Loveland, CO 80539.

More Resources for Your Children's Ministry

Quick Children's Sermons 2: Why Did God Make Mosquitoes?

Now you're ready to answer some of the most common questions kids ask about God…Jesus…heaven…and life as they observe it. You get 50 more befuddling questions straight from the lips of God's smallest saints…and great answers, too! Use this warm, witty book as a year's supply of children's sermons…for Sunday school… or to launch discussions in class or children's church!

ISBN 0-7644-2052-6

Smart Choices for Preteen Kids

Help your kids make good decisions with these 20 faith-building lessons. Plus, these relational lessons help kids form a solid, Christian support group—friends to encourage them during tough times. Your preteens will apply what they learn…and be better prepared to confront their teenage years. This book is a must for Sunday school teachers and leaders of 5th- and 6th-grade groups.

ISBN 0-7644-2039-9

More Smart Choices for Preteen Kids   ISBN 0-7644-2110-7

The Ultimate Bible Guide for Children's Ministry

You want your kids to know the difference between the Old and New Testaments. To quickly and easily find Bible verses. To understand the Bible and be comfortable exploring God's Word. Start here! These kid-friendly, 5- to 15-minute activities help children from preschool through 6th grade master the skills that make Bible reading fun. Give kids a rock-solid foundation for using the Bible, and do it without boring kids.

ISBN 0-7644-2076-3

Incredible Edible Bible Story Fun for Preschoolers

Jane Jarrell & Deborah Saathoff

Here are more than 40 favorite Bible stories, each with a recipe for an easy-make, tasty treat preschoolers will make themselves. Photocopiable recipe cards you can send home. You can use these recipes with your existing programs or build entire lessons by adding fun suggestions found in each activity!

ISBN 0-7644-2108-5

Order today from your local Christian bookstore, or write: Group Publishing, P.O. Box 485, Loveland, CO 80539.